farah

PROVINCIAL HANDBOOK / A Guide to the People and the Province

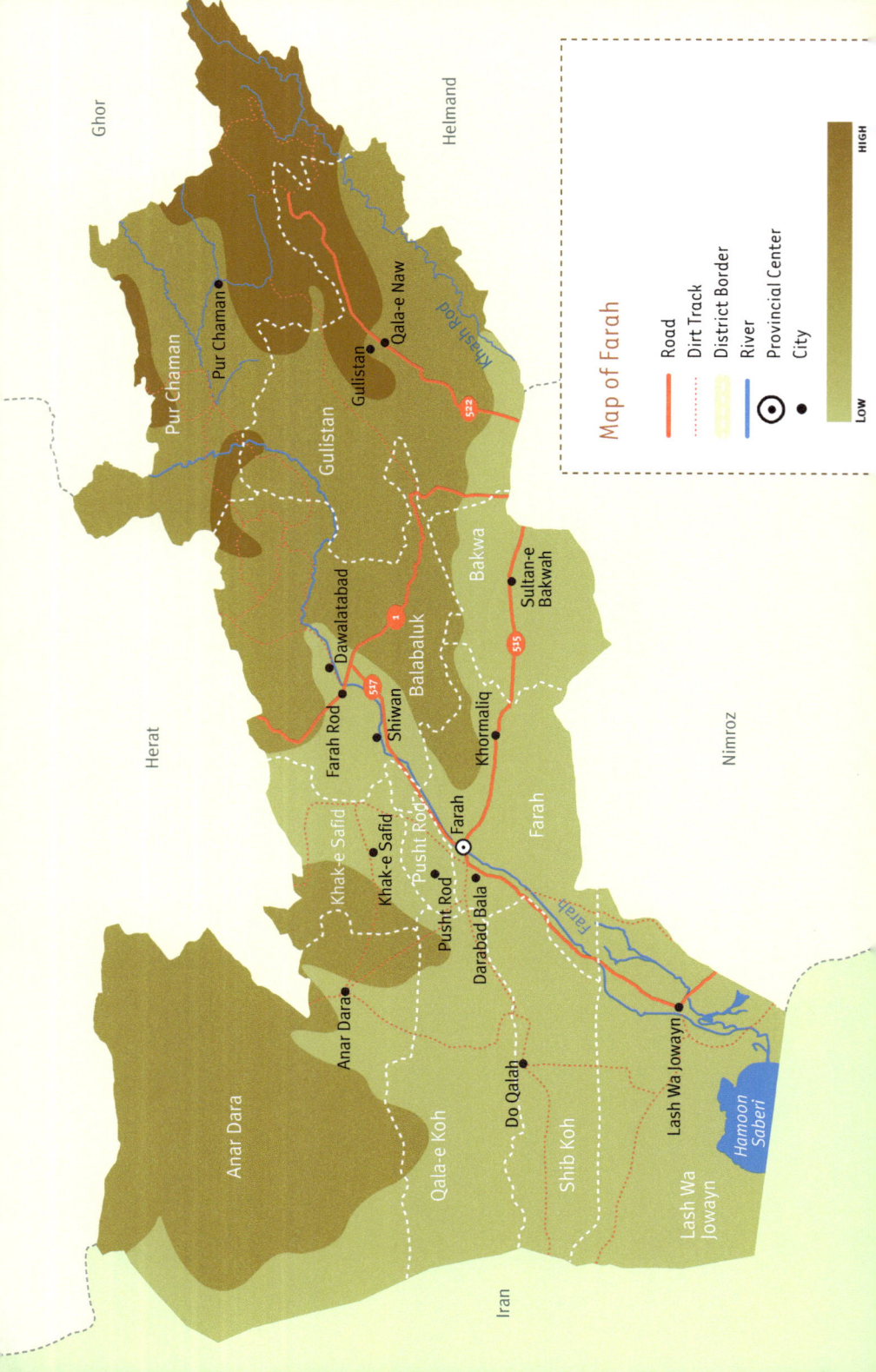

Table of Contents

Guide to the Handbook viii

Chapter 1: Overview and Orientation 1
    Orientation 4
    Relevant Historical Issues 8

Chapter 2: Ethnicity, Tribes, Language, and Religion 15
    Ethnicity 15
    Languages 16
    Role of Tribes 16
    Role of Religion 26

Chapter 3: Government and Leadership 29
    How the Government Officially Works 29
    How It Actually Works 31
    Security Forces 36
    Political Parties 39
    Leader Profiles 39

Chapter 4: The Economy 45
    Infrastructure 45
    Key Economic Sectors 49

Chapter 5: International Community and Reconstruction Activities. . . 53
    Provincial Reconstruction Team (PRT) 53
    National Solidarity Program (NSP) 54
    Projects and Activities 54
    International Organizations and the United Nations 61

Chapter 6: Information and Influence 65
    Telecommunications 66
    Media 66

Chapter 7: Big Issues 69
    Narcotics 69
    Taliban Insurgency 70
    Criminal Activity 73
    Police Reform 74
    Relations with Iran 75

Appendices 77
    Timeline of Events 77
    Common Compliments 78
    Common Complaints 78
    A Day in the Life of a Farahi 79
    Further Reading and Sources 80

List of Tables and Maps

LIST OF TABLES
Table 1. District Populations 6

Table 2. District Tribal Shuras 22

Table 3. Major Tribes in Farah 24

Table 4. Political Parties 38

Table 5. USAID Projects 60

Table 6. Other Development Activities 62

LIST OF MAPS
Map 1. Population Map of Nimroz 2

Map 2. Tribal Map of Nimroz 18

Map 3. Economic Map of Nimroz 46

Cover Photograph by Staff Sergeant Nicholas Pilch
Title Page Photograph by Master Sgt. Tracy DeMarco

Acronyms and Key Terms

ABP	Afghan Border Police	
ADT	Agribusiness Development Team	
ANA	Afghan National Army	
ANBP	Afghan National Border Police	
ANDS	Afghan National Development Strategy	
ANP	Afghan National Police	
ANSF	Afghan National Security Forces	
Arbakai	A volunteer, tribal police force which follows a strict ethical code	
AWCC	Afghan Wireless Communication Company	
BEFA	Basic Education for Afghanistan	
BPHS	Basic Package of Health Services	
CA	Civil Affairs	
CDCs	Community Development Councils	
CERP	Commander's Emergency Response Program	
CHC	Comprehensive Health Centers	
COIN	Counter Insurgency	
CSO	Central Statistics Office	
DDS	District Development Shuras	
DIAG	Disbandment of Illegal Armed Groups	
DoS	US Department of State	
DST	District Support Team	
FATA	Federally Administered Tribal Areas	
GIRoA	Government of the Islamic Republic of Afghanistan	
HIG or HIH	Hezb-e Islami Gulbuddin ("Islamic Party" formed by Gulbuddin Hekmatyar)	
HIK	Hezb-e Islami Khalis ("Islamic Party" formed by Mohammad Yunus Khalis)	

ICRC	International Committee of the Red Cross
IDLG	Independent Directorate for Local Governance
IED	Improvised Explosive Devices
IO	International Organization
IRoA	Islamic Republic of Afghanistan
ISAF	International Security Assistance Force
ISI	Inter-Service Intelligence (Pakistan)
Karez	A small underground irrigation system popular in Afghanistan
LGCD	Local Governance and Community Development Program
Meshrano Jirga	Elders' Assembly, upper house of Afghan National Assembly
MRRD	Ministry of Rural Rehabilitation and Development
Mustafiat	Department of Finance
NDS	National Directorate for Security
NGO	Non-Governmental Organization
NSP	National Solidarity Program
NWFP	North West Frontier Province
Pashtunwali	The Pashtuns' pre-Islamic code of conduct
PC	Provincial Council
PDC	Provincial Development Council
PDP	Provincial Development Plan
PRT	Provincial Reconstruction Team
UN	United Nations
UNAMA	United Nations Assistance Mission in Afghanistan
UNOPS	United Nations Office for Project Services
USACE	US Army Corp of Engineers
USAID	US Agency for International Development
USDA	US Department of Agriculture
Wali	Governor
Wolesi Jirga	People's Assembly, lower house of Afghan National Assembly
Woluswal	District Administrator

Guide to the Handbook

This handbook is a concise field guide to Farah for internationals deploying to the province. Field personnel have used these guides in Afghanistan since June 2008 to accelerate their orientation process and to serve as a refresher on different aspects of the province during their tour.

Reading this book will provide a basic understanding of the people, places, history, culture, politics, economy, needs, and ideas of Farah. Building upon this understanding can help you:

- Build rapport and a regular dialogue with local leaders.

- Plan and implement pragmatic strategies (security, political, economic) to address sources of instability.

- Influence communities to support the political process, not the insurgents.

- Build the capacity and legitimacy of a self-sufficient Afghan government and economy.

As you read the handbook and continue your inquiry in the province, seek to understand the influential leaders and groups in your local area and what beliefs and relationships drive their behavior. Think about the sources of violence in the area and whether groups are pursuing interests in a way that promotes conflict or stability. Finally, consider how various types of activities—key leader engagement, development assistance, security operations, security assistance, or public diplomacy—can effectively influence communities to work within the political process and oppose insurgency.

SOURCES AND METHODS

These handbooks are not intended as original academic research but as concise, readable summaries for practitioners in the field. The editorial team relies on its collective field experience and knowledge of the province as well as key sources, such as the official Islamic Republic of Afghanistan (IRoA), United Nations, and United States Government (USG) publications, and those sources listed in the appendix.

The editors made every effort to ensure accuracy, but there is often considerable disagreement regarding what is "ground truth" in Farah, and things are constantly changing. As such, consider this book part of your orientation, and not an all-inclusive source for everything you need to know.

Information in this handbook is unclassified. The views and opinions expressed in this handbook are those of IDS International and in no way reflect the views of the United States Government or the United States Army.

THE ELECTRONIC UPDATE

Look for electronic updates to this book at *www.idsinternational.net/afpakbooks*. Updates will cover new developments, issues, and leaders that emerge after publication. They will also provide corrections and expanded content in key areas based on input from readers.

We hope the handbook will continue to be a valuable tool in thinking about the challenges in Farah. If you have questions, comments, or feedback for future updates or editions please email *afpakbooks@idsinternational.net*.

ABOUT IDS INTERNATIONAL

Publisher of Afghanistan and Pakistan Provincial Handbooks Series

This book is part of a series of handbooks on Afghanistan and Pakistan provinces and regions. Afghanistan province titles include Nimroz, Nuristan, Kunar, Nangarhar, Laghman, Khost, Paktika, Ghazni, Paktya, Helmand, and Kandahar. Pakistan province titles include North West Frontier Province (NWFP) and the Federally Administered Tribal Areas (FATA).

In addition to publishing these handbooks, IDS International provides training and analysis to government and private organizations in the areas of politics, economics, culture, stability operations, reconstruction, counterinsurgency, and interagency relations. In particular, IDS is a leading trainer of the US military in working with Provincial Reconstruction Teams (PRTs) in Iraq and Afghanistan. IDS offers its clients expertise and experience in the difficult work of interagency collaboration in complex operations. The writers and editors on this project offer a lifetime of experience working in these provinces and share a dedication to bringing peace and prosperity to the people of Afghanistan.

Author: Carlo Antonio Nino
Editors: Nick Dowling and Saskia Funston
Assistant Editor: Tom Viehe
Reviewers: Gwen Cherne and Farid Ahmad Barkzai
Copy Editors: Michael Provenza, Emily Rose, and Gaye Newton

IDS INTERNATIONAL GOVERNMENT SERVICES
1916 Wilson Boulevard
Suite 302
Arlington, VA 22201
703-875-2212
www.idsinternational.net
afpakbooks@idsinternational.net

PUBLISHED: NOVEMBER 2010

© Copyright 2010 by IDS International Government Services LLC (IDS). All rights reserved.

This book (both digital and hard copy formats, including maps and updates) may not be reproduced in whole or in part, in any form, without written permission of IDS. This limitation includes email, printing copies, photocopying, or any other means of distribution or replication

This and other AfPak handbooks may be bought in either hard copy or digital format. Samples are available upon request. IDS International is also a leading provider of training and support or the cultural, political, economic, interagency and information aspects of conflict. For inquiries, please email afpakbooks@idsinternational.net or call 703-875-2212.

Farah City is the capital and largest city in Farah province. In the distance lies the "Citadel of Infidels," thought to be the remnants of the old town that was a strategic hub along the Silk Road.

PHOTO BY CARLO NINO

Chapter 1
Overview and Orientation

From the air, the human presence in Farah is barely noticeable. There are few trees or green areas, and a thin film of fine sand drifts across the province, twisting into sand storms that create mobile hills and occasional dust devils which locals believe are spirits trying to find their way home. The Farah River ("Farah Rod") cuts diagonally across the province and into a major lake shared with Iran called Hamoon Sabari. People farm close to the banks of the Farah River, but the river is often dry in the summer, forcing them to often rely on subsurface water. Other waterways like the Nizgan River, the Khash Rod River, and canals bring needed irrigation to crops of wheat, poppy, and some fruits. At the heart of the province is a flat, featureless capital built around a bustling bazaar. Rugs, jewelry, shawls, and imports from Iran and Pakistan can be found there. A single policeman directs traffic around the city's main roundabout, a structure which still bears the scars of recent insurgent attacks.

Farah is a rural province whose people base their lives on subsistence farming. With no effective water management, farmers irrigate their crops and orchards with runoff from melted snow. While wheat remains the crop of choice, many turn to poppy because it requires less water to grow. Other crops include cucumbers, watermelons, tomatoes, okra, and eggplants, with small amounts of alfalfa and grapes. Farah produces rugs, but little else; most consumer goods are imported from Iran or Pakistan.

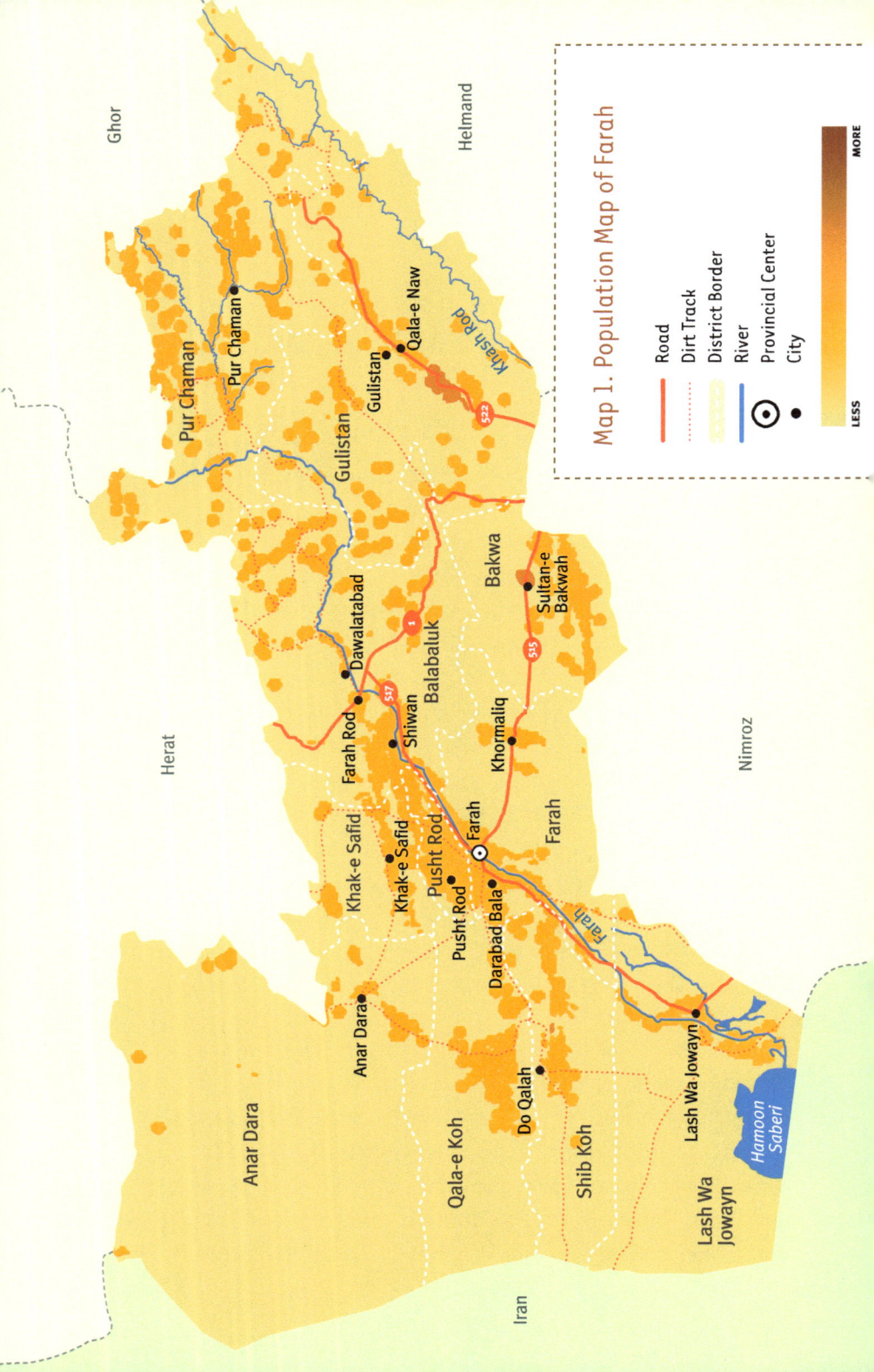

Farahi men often wear long shirts or contemporary Iranian business clothes. Lighter colors are worn during the spring and summer, while black, brown, dark green, or blue colors are worn during the fall and winter seasons. Older men will wear turbans which encircle a small brimless cap often called a *sindh*. Women often still wear full dress *burkhas* of black or blue that they begin to wear following puberty.

The majority of Farahi are Pashtuns, with a few Baluch, Tajik, Aimak, and other groups scattered throughout the province. The Pashtuns are mainly Durrani from the Zirak and Panj-pai branches. The two most prominent tribes are the Barakzai and Noorzai tribes. A few Kuchi (nomads) also live in the province, but their number depends on the season. A majority of people speak Pashto in the province, but Dari is also widely spoken.

Farah's residents suffer from economic marginalization and heightened criminal and insurgent activity. Many Pashtun residents lived in Iran during Afghanistan's wars. Returnees, including those annually deported from Iran, have struggled to find adequate employment in this manufacturing- and industry-poor province. Each year, many Farahis travel to Iran to work as manual laborers. The Taliban and other anti-government elements use these migrant workers and returning refugees as a base for recruitment.

ISAF's operations in Farah are controlled by the Italian-led Regional Command West in Herat. A small ISAF contingent consisting of Italian troops is based near the airport in Farah City next to the US Provincial Reconstruction Team (PRT) complex. The US PRT also has a small Afghan National Army (ANA) contingent inside the complex.

ORIENTATION

Farah province is one of the westernmost provinces in Afghanistan. It is bordered by Helmand in the south, Nimroz in the southwest, Herat in the north, Ghor in the northeast, and Iran in the west. In terms of territory, it is the fourth largest province in the country, with an area of about 480,000 square kilometers. Farah is largely undeveloped and sparsely populated. The Central Statistics Office estimates that around 493,000 people live in the province, although there has not been a census in the country since 1979. About 90 percent of the population lives in rural districts.

The center and west of the province is generally flat desert land with low hills. These gradually give way to the mountains in the eastern districts, which rise up to 13,000 feet. Most of the cultivated areas lie close to the Farah River, and large plots of cultivated land in southern Bakwa district rely exclusively on subsurface water. Unfortunately, without a regular water source, some of the most arable land in Farah remains barren. Officially, the province is divided into 11 districts—the provincial capital and district of Farah, Pusht Rod, Anar Dara, Shib Koh, Qala-e Koh, Lash Wa Juwayn, Khak-e Safid, Bala Baluk, Bakwa, Gulistan, and Pur Chaman. Farah City is the provincial capital, and its district has an estimated population of about 102,400 inhabitants.

Because of its elevation (about 2,900 feet), Farah has a very mild and pleasant winter with only one month in which temperatures drop below freezing at night (to about 20 degrees Fahrenheit) and rise to 30 to 40 degrees Fahrenheit in the day. Snow has fallen only a few times in the past ten years. By contrast, summers are extremely hot and dry, with daytime temperatures getting up to 150 degrees Fahrenheit in July and August. Farah receives about three inches of rain per year, primarily in the spring. In May, June, July, and August a heavy wind called the *Badi Yaw Sal Shal Roza* blows. This wind creates sand storms that block roads, cover bazaars, and sometimes even destroy crops in vulnerable areas. The sandstorms range from billowy clouds to outright horizontal bursts of sand.

Districts

Like much of the Afghan rural population, the people of Anar Dara are conservative Muslims. Mullahs have a great deal of influence in this district. The Taliban did not treat the locals very well during their reign and are still viewed poorly. But locals in Anar Dara believe that the international community has wasted many resources which could have been used to implement development projects through the Ministry of Reconstruction and Rural Development.

The Taliban are not welcome in Shib Koh; they are seen as bringing insecurity with them. Locals are very sensitive to the presence of foreigners, and are often critical of ISAF for carrying out operations without consulting local leaders.

Lash Wa Juwayn is the most ethnically diverse district in Farah. Some villages have Pashtuns, Ellat, Tajiks, and Surkhkaman living side by side. While locals support the government, they are critical of the rampant corruption. Still, they believe that the government, not the international community, should be in charge of implementing development projects.

Pur Chaman is a Tajik- and Aimak-dominated district that borders very insecure areas in Bala Baluk and Gulstan districts of Farah province, as well as the Pashtun-dominated Helmand and Ghor provinces. The Tajik and Aimak often resist intimidation from the Taliban, who enter their territory from neighboring provinces.

Table 1: District Populations

District	Center	Population	Major Tribes and Ethnicities
Farah	Farah City	109,409	Noorzai, Barakzai, Alizai, Alokazai, Isakzai, Tajiks
Pusht Rod	Pusht Rod	36,315	Noorzai, Isakzai, Barakzai
Khak-e Safid	Khak-e Safid	34,600	Noorzai, Achakzai
Qala-e Koh	Qala-e Koh	30,653	Noorzai, Barakzai, Alizai, Baluch
Shib Koh	Shib Koh	23,013	Barakzai, Popolzai, Tajik
Bala Baluk	Shiwan	72,465	Noorzai, Alizai, Barakzai, Achakzai
Anar Dara	Anar Dara	24,782	Isakzai, Alizai, Noorzai, Baluch,
Bakwa	Sultan-e Bakwa	39,871	Noorzai
Lash Wa Juwayn	Lash Wa Juwayn	20,499	Isakzai, Noorzai, Popolzai, Tajik, Ellat, Sourkh-Kaman
Gulistan	Gulistan	49,774	Noorzai, Barakzai
Pur Chaman	Pur Chaman	51,626	Tajik, Aimak, Magul, Ellat
Total		493,007	

CSO/UNFPA Socio Economic and Demographic Profile

Many of the smaller ethnic groups in Pur Chaman are also very independent, and they fear Pashtuns from neighboring areas. The perceived threat from Pashtuns helps bring peoples of Pur Chaman together.

Key Towns

The town of **Farah** is the capital of the province. It is small, with an unpaved airstrip and one paved road. Low, modern buildings stand alongside hardened dried mud walls giving the city a flat, featureless profile. Small cars, motorbikes, and trucks hauling bricks and other miscellaneous items clamor through the narrow streets. Walls along the road are covered with posters and electoral signs, including many from bygone elections. The town is oriented around the marketplace, where one can find practically anything among the mixture of CDs, Pakistani and Iranian items, and processed food. On the outskirts of town, new living quarters are being built next to above ground cemeteries where graves are marked by headstones and brightly colored strips of cloth.

Chien Farsi is considered the de facto capital of Pusht Rod district. The population prospers by producing tools, masonry, seeds, small goods, and foodstuffs. Two roads connect the city to the rest of the province; one travels to Route 517, which in turn connects to Route 1 or the "Ring Road," and one travels south to Farah City.

Chien Farsi's sister city, **Masow**, is similar in composition but lies about 30 kilometers to the west. It has a road traveling south to Farah City, but lacks a road to Route 1. The PRT plans to initiate a road project in December 2010 to connect Masow and Chien Farsi.

The capital of Bala Baluk, **Shiwan**, has been the center of conflict in the province since 2007. The government is small and struggles to maintain its legitimacy. They send representation to Farah City frequently and maintain a close relationship with their neighbors in Pusht Rod. Tribes around Shiwan are well known for their rug weaving using local looms.

Qala-e Naw is a small village in Gulistan district with only about 100 residents. While similar to many of its neighboring villages, Qala-e Naw is significant because it lies upstream on the Murghab (a small tributary of the Khash Rod River). It has the power to divert the flow of water to communities lying to the south. The population of Qala-e Naw grows poppy in several of the fields around the village.

RELEVANT HISTORICAL ISSUES

From Ancient to Modern Times

Identified as the ancient towns of Phrada, Prophtasia, or Phra, the old town of Farah is said to have stood on the right bank of the Farah River where the "Citadel of the Infidels" or "Citadel of Farah" still stands today. Locals believe the citadel is the remnants of the old town center before the town moved to the left bank of the river. While legend (almost certainly apocryphal) dates its foundation to the time of Alexander the Great, others claim it is only 200 years old. It was allegedly used by the Soviet artillery as a test site. Today it is largely home to opium addicts.

Farah's strategic location helped to protect the eastern border of the early Sassanid Empire and served as a main point along trade

routes between the Levant and India. It continued to thrive through
several Persian empires, the conquest of Alexander the Great, and
the Sassanid Empire. The invasion of Genghis Khan brought a long
period of chaos and decline to Farah. The same strategic location
which had brought it success now made it a focal point for conflict.
Between the 10th and 19th centuries, the city was taken and
pillaged many times, ruining its majesty.

In 1862, Dost Mohammed Khan seized Farah from the Persian Empire,
and the city and surrounding area became a part of modern-day
Afghanistan. Because of its recent addition to the country, Farah still
has many Persian customs and is seen by Iran to be an essential
part of its history. Between 1870 and 1872, British telegraph workers
surveyed and demarcated what is now Iran's border with Afghanistan
along Nimroz and Farah provinces. Iranian officials disagreed with the
survey results, which they believed unjustly awarded Iranian territory
to Afghanistan, but Iran in the late nineteenth century was too weak
to do more than protest.

In 1965, the Kandahar-Herat segment of Highway 1 (also known
as "the Ring Road") was opened, bypassing the city of Farah. As a
result, the city lost its traditional role as a main commercial transit
stop and began to once again decline.

Communist Era (1978-1992)

In 1978, army officers loyal to the Khalq faction of the Communist
Party stormed the palace and killed President Mohammad Daoud.
Known as the Saur Revolution, this coup d'etat brought Nur
Mohammad Taraki to power. Seeking to cement their power and
undermine religious opposition, the new government ordered the
arrest and murder of a number of religious opponents in early

1979. Pir Bahauddin Jan, the last of the Naqshbandi Sufi leaders of the Aimak in Pur Chaman, was among those killed in the purges.

Nearly a year later, the Soviet Union invaded and occupied Afghanistan, putting a rival faction of the Communist Party in charge of the country. The Soviets, invading from the north, quickly moved through Herat to occupy the strategic city of Farah. As a result, Farah was host to several fierce battles between Soviet forces and mujahedin groups. Harakat-e Inqilab-e Islami, Sharafat Kuh Front, and Jamiat-e Islami were the dominant mujahedin factions during the Soviet war. Allegiance to the groups broke down along linguistic lines—Dari-speakers joined the Jamiat-e Islami and Pashto-speakers joined the Harakat. The ongoing war caused around 45 percent of the pre-war population to migrate to neighboring Iran as refugees. The war also left Farah as one of the most heavily mined provinces in the country.

During its occupation of Afghanistan, the Soviet Union made several improvements to the city, including an expeditionary airfield, a bridge known as Garden's Bridge, and a two-story building just north of the city. They also constructed Routes 515 and 517 in order to connect Farah to the rest of the country via the Ring Road.

Mujahedin and the Taliban (1992-2001)

Following the withdrawal of Soviet troops and the overthrow of the communist government, Afghanistan was divided between various mujahedin groups. Based in the southern city of Kandahar, the Taliban quickly began to consolidate control of the country. While their attempts to seize Kabul in March 1995 failed, they were able to take control of Nimroz province that year and began advancing on Farah and Herat. Isma'il Khan, a Tajik mujahedin leader in Herat, and Burhanuddin Rabbani of Jamiat-e Islami led the provinces in fierce battles against the Taliban. In April the Taliban successfully captured Farah. But Rabbani and Khan's forces led a counter-attack, driving the Taliban back into Helmand. In Gereshk, Ismail Khan's forces were defeated. The Taliban quickly took back northern Helmand and pushed into Farah. In September Ismail Khan abandoned Shindand in southern Herat and fled to Iran, ceding control of Farah and Herat to the Taliban.

Once the Taliban took control of Farah, they closed all the schools and required boys to attend *madrassas,* which taught the religious interpretations and political ideology of the Taliban. Women were not permitted out of their home without a *hijab* and an escort. Several mullahs critical of the Taliban were arrested and tortured, such as Munshia Abib in Pusht Rod and Rauufi in Qala-e Koh. These mullahs were replaced by acolytes of the Taliban who used this process to assume control of religious leaders in the province.

Though drug smuggling and organized crime flourished, many people in the province remember the time as one of security. The Taliban confiscated all the pistols and rifles in the province, which many people believe made the neighborhoods safer.

Mullah Baz Muhammad, the sub-governor of Shindand district in Herat, became popular in Farah during this time due to his sympathetic attitude towards the people. He regularly met with the population, made himself available, did not denounce education, and was not seen as harsh. As a result, when the Taliban fell, Mullah Baz Muhammad was able to find refuge in Farah as a Taliban leader who continues to fight coalition forces.

Contemporary Events (2001-present)

The Taliban government in Farah surrendered after a US aerial assault, and, although many inactive Talibs remained in the province, Taliban activity was low for several years. Local mujahedin and technocrats took over key positions within the provincial administration, but many of them were corrupt and contributed to criminal and Taliban activity in the province. Farah had six governors between 2001 and the current administration—Engineer Abdul Hai Nemati, Bashir Baghlani, Engineer Asadullah Fallah, Ezattullah Wasefi, Abdul Samad Estanakzai, and Moheuddin Baluch—but each was believed to be corrupt and helping the Taliban gain a foothold in the province. Similarly, the police chiefs have either been corrupt (as in the case of the first two police chiefs, Zabet Jabil and General Amir Mohammad) or inept. In many cases, the weakness of the government in Farah has been due to the lack of training and knowledge.

As early as 2005, Pur Chaman and Gulistan had become a hub for Taliban members fleeing Helmand. The Taliban hold on Farah tightened through 2006 as the insurgency gained greater control of Helmand, and by 2006 the Taliban were occupying entire districts of Farah and murdering government officials across the Pashtun districts of Bala Baluk, Khak-e Safid, and Bakwa. Several campaigns have been launched to clear Taliban forces out of these districts, but after each operation the Taliban have been able to creep back in.

In March 2008 Rohul Amin was appointed governor and has quickly gained a reputation as a hardliner against the Taliban. Afghan and ISAF troops launched a campaign in late 2009 into the stronghold of Taliban territory in Bala Baluk. In October, they succeeded in capturing the Taliban's headquarters in Shiwan, Bala

Baluk. Once again, however, the insurgency has rebounded, this time due to an influx of fighters pushed out of Helmand by ISAF operations in Helmand during 2010.

Multiple shadow governors of the Taliban have been in charge of Farah since 2001. Mowlavi Abdul Rahman, Mullah Baz Muhammad, and Mullah Rasul each served in this role and were either killed by ISAF troops or supplanted by rivals. The last, Mullah Rasul, was facing investigation by the Taliban leadership in Quetta, Pakistan for providing information to coalition forces that led to the deaths of Mullah Naik Mohammad and Mullah Abdul Manan, both key insurgent commanders in Bala Baluk. Since Rasul's death, Mullah Zaqir has taken over as the main Taliban leader in Farah province and is thought of as the current shadow governor. Following the resurgence of the Taliban in 2006, the Farah insurgency has struggled with infighting, challenges of communication and coordination with leadership in Pakistan, and significant ISAF disruption of operations. However, since Mullah Zaqir took over, Taliban infighting has decreased and the different leaders have started to coordinate operations.

Soldiers gather with respected elders to establish and maintain a trusting relationship. Pashtun tribes are the largest ethnic group in Farah. Tribal disputes over land, water, and other resources have caused conflict over the years. Tajik, Baluch, Ellat, Surkhkaman, Hazara, and Kuchi live in Farah.

PHOTO BY LANCE CPT. JOHN HITESMAN

Chapter 2
Ethnicity, Tribes, Languages, and Religion

Afghan society is made up of interlocking and overlapping networks of affiliations, families, and occupations. Such a network is referred to as a *qawm*. Every individual belongs to a qawm which provides cooperation, support, security, and assistance in social, political, or economic situations. Frequently a village corresponds to a qawm, which is more than a geographic location. In a more restricted sense, qawm refers to social groups, from family kin to an ethnic group. In tribal areas qawm refers to a common genealogy from extended family or clan, to tribe or tribal confederation. Most simply, qawm defines an individual's identity in his social world.

ETHNICITY

Pashtuns are the dominant ethnic group in Farah, making up 80 percent of the population. Some Tajiks, most of whom migrated to Farah from Yazd, Iran, live around the capital city. They call their small part of the city *Yazdi*. Tajiks live around Farah City and are also found in Gulistan and Pur Chaman districts. In total, Tajiks make up 14 percent of the population. Some Aimaks and Hazara are scattered throughout the province, and a small number of Baluch are concentrated in the south. The number of Kuchis (nomads) in Farah varies depending on the season.

LANGUAGES

Each ethnicity speaks its own language; Pashtuns speak Pashto, Tajiks speak Persian or Dari, and Baluch speak Baluchi. Some people are fluent in several languages. About 84 percent and 50 percent of the population speak Pashto and Dari, respectively. Baluchi is spoken in only four villages.

ROLE OF TRIBES

Tribes in Farah are known to feud with each other over the division of resources, such as land and water. These tribal disputes can turn violent and are sometimes exploited by the insurgency. In some cases, insurgent groups have sided with one party in an argument, offering it protection or resources. In the absence of functional government courts, tribes rely on their leadership to arbitrate a mutual agreement. When these leaders fail to resolve their differences, insurgent groups have been able to exploit sentiments to their own advantage. Often opinions about the insurgency or the Afghan government are shaped by these local disputes and politics. For example, in the Bala Baluk district, the Alizai tribe has increasingly sided with insurgent groups, and local disputes with the Noorzai and Barakzai tribes have been strong motivational factors. Most of the local disputes are centered on the ownership of local estuaries and their ability to cultivate and irrigate farmland.

An anthropological textbook would describe the tribe as the most powerful facet of Pashtun society. It provides an informal governmental framework. Tribal society works on a group, rather than an individual, decision-making structure. All decisions for the tribe or sub-sections within a tribe are determined as a group by the tribal elders, who tend to be local *khans* (large landowners) and *maliks* (influential community leaders with quasi-official status). The goal of justice is to promote group harmony, rather than to punish an individual.

There are two primary mechanisms for tribal elders to make decisions. The first is called a *jirga*, which is a meeting held to make a specific decision. Any decision made in a jirga is binding.

The other meeting type is called a *shura*, from the Arabic word for consultation. Shuras seek to redress wrongs through arbitration, and address issues of pride and reparations more than they actually impose punishment. After decades of war, shuras have become more militarized in Afghanistan, acting as short-term advisory councils that can include elders, commanders, and landowners. Shuras re-emerged as a viable local governance structure upon the fall of the Taliban.

Tribal relations are complex and have a direct impact on stability. There is some dispute regarding the extent to which tribal affiliations can be used as an indicator of an individual's disposition towards the Afghan government and coalition forces. While the Alizai and Noorzai tribes may provide the majority of recruits to the Taliban, and the Barakzai and Achakzai tribes may be more closely affiliated with the central government, tribal affiliations are not accurate ways to determine political allegiance. Loyalties can and often do shift in Afghanistan.

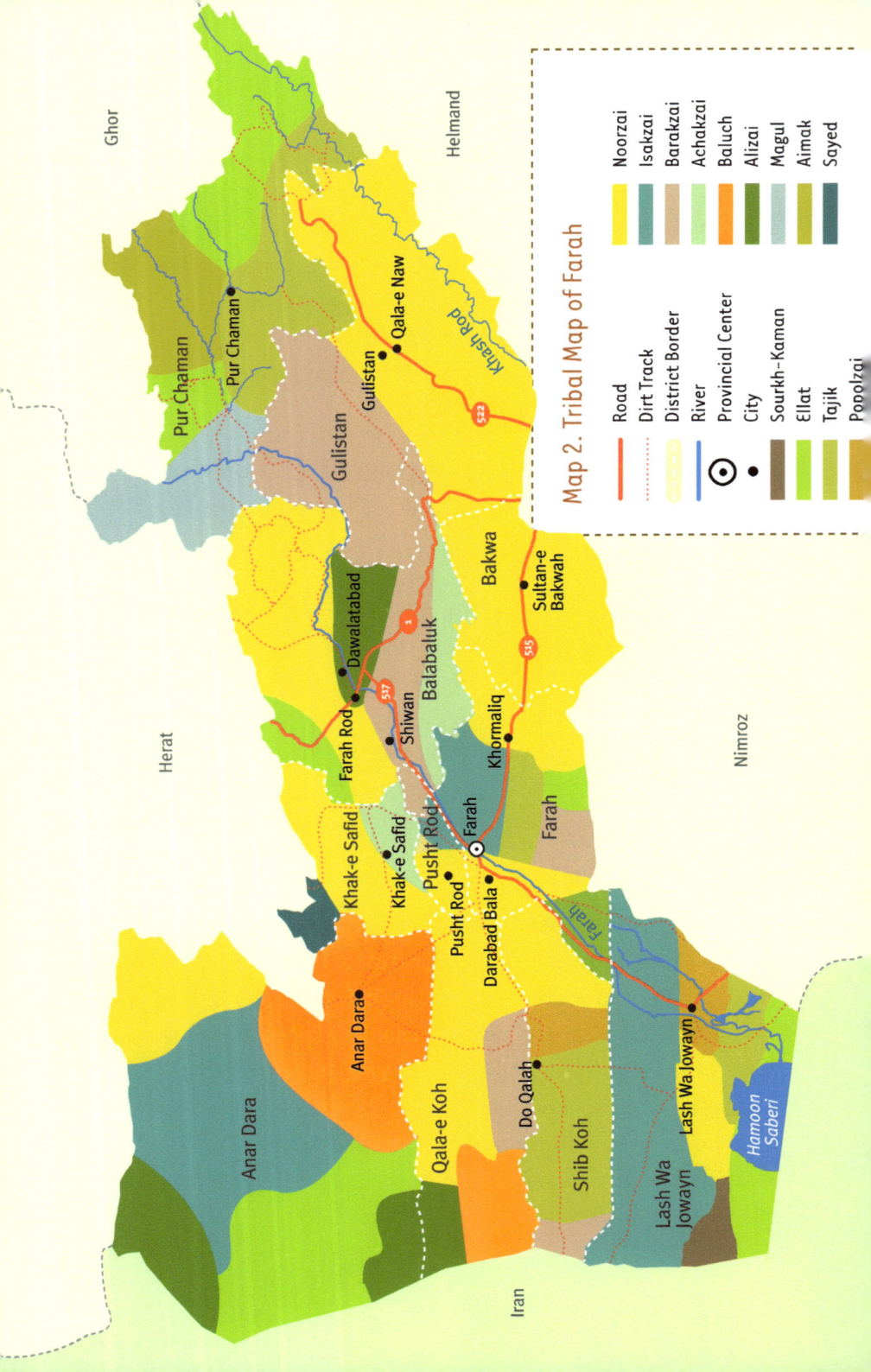

Farah's Pashtuns share many close ethnic links to tribes in Helmand province, which provides a conduit for the migration of the insurgency. Also, Farah's Noorzai have links with the Shindand district of Herat, including the pro- and anti-government elements. These ties do not definitively characterize or quantify support for the Taliban, but rather show the range of tribal and political allegiances at play in just one province of Afghanistan. The context is further complicated when the number and dynamics of sub-tribes are considered.

Due to several social and political upheavals, many of the tribes have feuds with each other and have often used their positions of influence to outright discredit other tribes. In practice many of the tribes have remained true to their original ancestry despite assuming characteristics or claims to larger tribal associations.

Pashtunwali

Nang (Honor): All parts of pashtunwali lead to Honor. All Pashtuns are required to uphold the honor of their family and their tribe by following the other parts of the code. An insult to someone's tribe or family can lead to Badal (revenge). Disrespect for the hospitality of another can also lead to Badal. The biggest disputes are over women, land, and money. A Pashtun man must protect these three with his life and honor.

Melmastia (Hospitality): Pashtuns are known for their hospitality and will go to great lengths to treat their guests with honor and respect. Most villages will have a dedicated guesthouse, and larger families will have their own. Even if the family has barely any resources, a stranger will be welcomed in, fed, and given a place to sleep. This applies to non-Pashtuns as well.

Nanawatay (Sanctuary): If one Pashtun has insulted another, or committed some crime, they may admit their guilt and ask for forgiveness. A gift of equivalent value to the debt incurred by the offender must be offered in conjunction with the request that the past be forgotten. The insulted party is then obligated to accept their offer. Nanawatay can also be used to beg for mercy and protection.

Badal (Revenge): Pashtuns are quick to take revenge for an insult, or seek justice for a past crime. It doesn't matter if the insult is decades old. Honor was taken away, and the only way to restore honor to the family/clan/tribe is to exact revenge on the other family/clan/tribe.

Namus (Honor of Women): Pashtuns defend the honor of Pashtun women from verbal and physical harm at all costs.

Prominent Pashtun Tribes of Farah

Pashtuns in Farah belong to the Durrani confederation or "super-tribe." Two large sub-branches—the **Panj-pai** and the **Zirak**—are prominent in the province. The Panj-pai (or "Five Fingers") presence in Farah is mostly comprised of Noorzai, Alizai, and Isakzai tribes. The Zirak are made up of the Barakzai, Alokazai, and Achakzai tribes. Zirak sometimes claim that the Noorzai tribe is from the Ghilzai confederation—historical rivals to the Durrani.

The **Alizai** around Bala Baluk's district center have longstanding disputes with both the Noorzai and Barakzai. On August 6, 2009, insurgents from the Alizai tribe arrested **Achakzai** tribesmen near Shiwan. In response, the Achakzai tribe arrested Alizai tribesmen near Kanask. Leaders from both tribes met along with the Director of Borders and Tribal Affairs and were able to resolve the dispute within three days.

The **Barakzai** people are Durrani Pashtuns and among the most well-regarded tribes in the country. They have produced a string of kings for the Afghan monarchy and continue to play an active and influential role in Afghan politics today.

The **Noorzai**, Durrani Pashtuns from the Panj-pai sub-branch, have a longstanding feud with Arabs who live in Anar Dara district. The Arabs were reportedly treated better by the Taliban, leading to the Noorzais' resentment. The Noorzai now have better standing in the district government than the Arabs and overtly wield their power over the Arabs. Noorzais also have had a historic conflict with the Achakzai, though their relations have improved significantly over the past few years.

Other Important Peoples

The **Aimak** are a Persian-speaking nomadic or semi-nomadic tribe of mixed Iranian and Mongolian descent who inhabit the north and northwest highlands of Afghanistan and the Khorasan province of Iran. They are mostly found in Ghor province, but many live in Pur Chaman district of Farah. They live in dwellings which closely resemble Mongolian-style yurts—a portable home with a circular wooden frame that is covered in felt. Unlike their Turco-Mongolian kinsmen in other areas, the Aimak speak Dari, a Persian dialect. Sufism grew in popularity in Aimak territory beginning in the 1970s, but their *pir*, or spiritual leader, was killed in 1979 as part of a communist purge of religious leaders.

The **Ellat** live in Farah district and Shib Koh. They are Sunni Muslim, originally from Iran, and speak Farsi. Most Ellats work in butchery and animal husbandry, and many are involved in the Jamiat-e Islami political party. The leader of the Ellat is Abdul Ghani Turabi, who serves as the Director of the Customs Department in Farah. The **Surkhkaman** are

Table 2: District Tribal Shuras

District	No. of members	Shura Leader	Notes
Anar Dara	8	Haji Ibrahim Jan	Tribal leaders discuss the security situation, reconstruction, and seek resolution to general disputes.
Bakwa	6	Haji Abdul Qadir	This shura meets as needs arise. The shura discusses and addresses issues surrounding the security situation, poverty, unity, and reconstruction in the district.
Bala Baluk	0	No district-level Shura	Bala Baluk does not have a tribal shura which holds regular meetings, but there are tribal leader meetings as needed. If problems arise between tribes at the district level, they are usually referred to tribal leadership.
Farah City	N/A	N/A	There is one Shura-e Shahri (town council) in the provincial capital. Its membership is primarily drawn from traders and shopkeepers. They meet on an irregular basis when and as issues arise.
Gulistan	0	No district-level Shura	Gulistan does not have a well-organized shura, so if issues do arise, the tribal leaders come together to make a decision. But this procedure is limited to the areas close to the district administration. Tribal leaders claim that in the remote areas of the district, around 80 percent of the disputes are resolved through Taliban courts.

District	No. of members	Shura Leader	Notes
Khak-e Safid	N/A	N/A	The tribal shura of Khak-e Safid functions as a representative body for arbitration among the district residents. It meets on an irregular basis in order to discuss people's disputes and seek solutions. The decisions that the tribal shura make are perceived as sound and binding by most of the locals.
Lash Wa Juwayn	17	Haji Malim Anwar Khan	This shura meets regularly to resolve issues between people as they arise.
Pur Chaman	N/A	Mawlavi Shah Muhammad	The main functions of this shura are maintaining unity among the various ethnic groups living in the district, resolving conflicts, and discussing reconstruction and security issues in the district. It meets as needed.
Pusht Rod	0	No district-level Shura	There is no shura at the district level, yet each tribe has its own council, which at times meets with other sub-tribal shuras to address the most pressing inter-tribal problems as they arise.
Qala-e Koh	4	Abdul Rahim Raufi	N/A
Shib Koh	52	Haji Abdul Hafiz	This joint shura, led by a Tajik with a Barakzai tribesmen serving as a deputy, meets once a month. Its main functions are resolving disputes, maintaining unity, strengthening security, and facilitating the implementation of development projects.

Table 3: Major Tribes in Farah

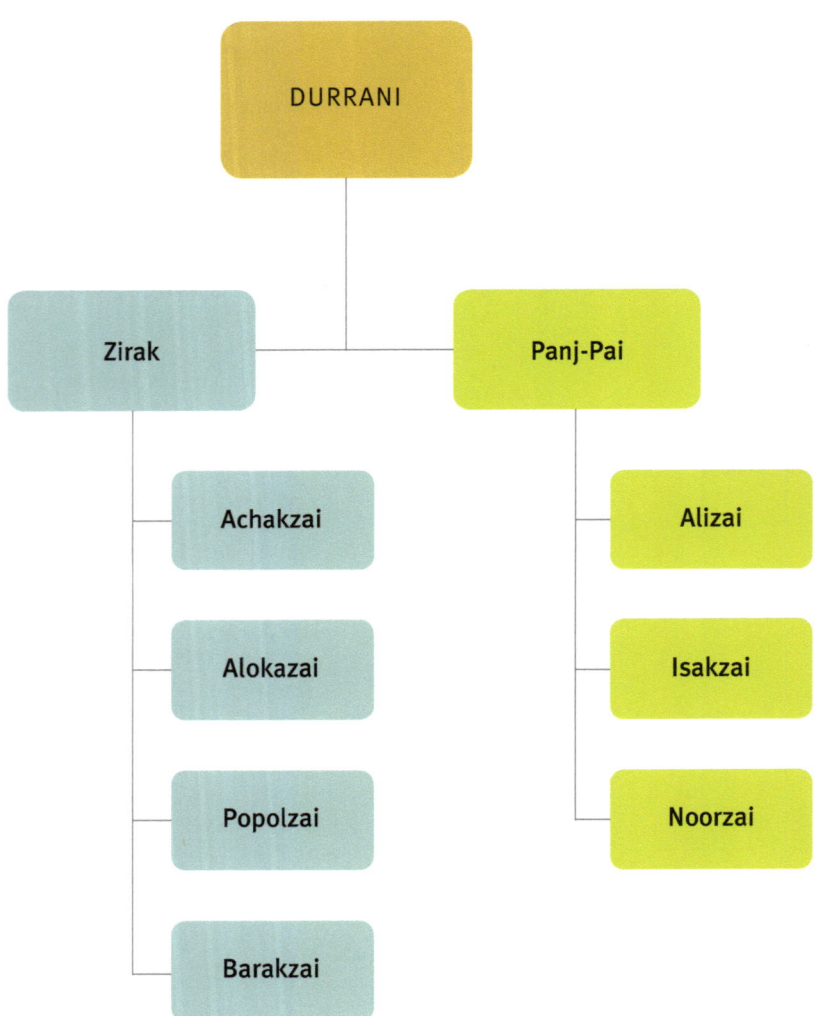

Sunni Muslims who live alongside their brother tribe, the Ellat. They are principally from Iran and live in Farah district. Muhammed Anwar, the district governor of Shib Koh, is the leader of the Surkhkaman.

There are no accurate figures on the number of **Kuchis** in the province, but it is estimated that around 25,000 Kuchi families live in Farah, out of which 18,600 families are registered. Migratory Kuchis may either be short- or long-term occupants of a place, depending on their migration pattern. In the summer, most of the Kuchis go to Ghor province, the Shindand district of Herat, or to the Pur Chaman district of Farah province. In the winter, most Kuchis move to the Khak-e Safid, Lash Wa Juwayn, Bakwa, Qala-e Koh, and Anar Dara districts of Farah province. Kuchis have good relations with locals throughout the province, though in parts of Anar Dara and Lash Wa Juwayn, as well as in the Rabat area of Khak-e Safid district, locals sometimes try to stop Kuchis from using local pastures. These lands are owned by the Afghan government, which authorizes the Kuchis to graze there.

District Tribal Shuras

The district tribal shuras vary in terms of necessity and presence. In Bala Baluk, for instance, there is no standing shura; one is convened when an event occurs that necessitates arbitration. Nevertheless, the government has a designated shura representative for each district whether it has a standing body or not. District shuras have faced a number of challenges, from mitigating tribal power to avoiding being targeted by the insurgency. Both formal and informal shuras acknowledge one another's activities, and members are often selected from the informal shura to serve on the government-sponsored shura. As a result, the selection of governmental shura members has at times lent itself to careerism, cronyism, and nepotism. A list of the district tribal shuras can be found in Table 2.

ROLE OF RELIGION

Islam is a central, pervasive influence throughout Afghan society and is totally intertwined with the activities of each day. The Afghan constitution states explicitly that no laws will be enacted that contradict Sharia law. The mullahs also play a role in village legal proceedings, thus further intertwining religion, law, and governance. Individual and family status depends on the proper observance of the society's value system based on concepts defined in Islam. These are characterized by honesty, frugality, generosity, virtuousness, piousness, fairness, truthfulness, tolerance, and respect for others.

The mosque is the center of religious life in rural Farah province. It is both a holy place and a community center. Smaller community-maintained mosques stand at the center of villages as well as town and city neighborhoods. The size of a village is often described by the number of mosques it has. Mosques serve not only as places of worship, but as a shelter for guests, a place to meet and gossip, and the focus of social religious festivities, and schools. Almost every Afghan man has studied at a mosque school or madrassa. For many, especially in rural Farah, this is the only formal education they receive.

The mullah is the spiritual leader of the village. He traditionally settles disputes like a judge and plays the role of teacher in the absence of a formal education system in the village. Some mullahs are barely literate or are only slightly more educated than the people they serve. Mullahs are normally appointed by the government after consultation with their communities and, although partially financed by the government, are largely dependent on community contributions for their livelihood, including shelter and a portion of the harvest. Supposedly versed in the Koran, Sunna, Hadith, and Sharia, they are charged with teaching the members of their community the fundamentals of Islamic ritual and behavior.

The majority of the mullahs stand behind the tribes. If the tribes make a decision, they often enjoy the support of the mullahs in the mosques. The Taliban do not directly influence the mullahs in these communities. Mullahs are often sympathetic toward the Taliban and will often take positions on political issues. Mullahs normally do not outright castigate or condemn the Taliban.

The Ministry of Rural Rehabilitation and Development (MRRD) estimates that the province is 95 percent Sunni and five percent Shia. The division between Shia and Sunni is largely based on ethnicity and tribe. While disputes arise between two separate religious groups in Farah, religion is not the source of the dispute. Instead, the dispute will be between two qawms, tribes, or ethnicities.

Governor Rohul Amin (third from the left) meets with US and Afghan officials. Governor Amin was appointed governor in March 2008 and has quickly gained a reputation as a hardliner against the Taliban. Nevertheless, the provincial government has had trouble establishing its legitimacy throughout the province.

PHOTO BY SENIOR AIRMAN RYLAN K. ALBRIGHT

Chapter 3
Government and Leadership

HOW THE GOVERNMENT OFFICIALLY WORKS

Central Control

Authority and power in Afghanistan are concentrated in the national government as a means to counter the power of warlords in the provinces. As such, the provincial government is limited to an advisory role for the central government, while decisions on everything from policy to funding priorities are made in Kabul.

Provincial Government

A governor (*wali*) heads the provincial government and reports to the Independent Directorate for Local Governance (IDLG) located in the Executive Office of the president. He is not elected, but is appointed by IDLG. The governor is assisted by a deputy and several staff who oversee provincial government management. Ministries in Kabul, with the approval of the president, appoint provincial line directors to execute their policies and programs at departments in each province. The directors report to and receive funds from the ministry in Kabul. The provincial governor has neither authority to appoint provincial line directors nor budgetary authority over any of these departments, but must approve all expenditures before they are processed by the Department of Finance (*Mustafiat*).

While the appointment process of both the governor and the department directors was conceived to reduce potential corruption and abuse of power, it often makes it difficult for the people to feel connected to their government officials. It also creates tension between the governor and line directors.

The Provincial Council (PC), the only elected body at the provincial level, provides an advisory voice for the people on provincial issues. The PC reports directly to the president but has no budget. Its relevance is largely dependent on the governor's support and its members' individual resources, influence, and initiatives.

The governor and provincial line directors sit on the Provincial Development Committee (PDC), which is responsible for creating the Provincial Development Plan (PDP) and coordinating development needs with key players in the province. UN organizations, the PRT, and interested NGOs also attend meetings. The PDP provides a vision for development within the province and includes a comprehensive list of projects that have been prioritized by the PDC. The list of projects in the PDP should include all those projects to be completed by GIRoA, PRT, USAID, NGO, UN, and other partners in the province. The PDP must be approved by the PC and in Kabul before projects can be implemented at the provincial level.

District and Local Governance

Government at the district level mirrors the provincial government with the *woluswal* (referred to as the district governor, district chief, district administrator, or sub-governor), police chief, National Directorate of Security (NDS) officer, clerks, and a small police force. Ministry sub-departments also operate at the district level through representatives, but are not present in every district. In 2007 District Development Assemblies (DDAs) were formed to plan, prioritize, and coordinate development activities at the district level. Below the district level, the only formal governance structures are the Community Development Councils (CDCs).

Some villages have established CDCs under the National Solidarity Program. The CDC is responsible for prioritizing and articulating the development needs of the community to the Afghan government and to the international donor community. Normally, CDCs elect a representative to sit on a DDA and interface with the district governor. Elected by the villagers, the CDC generally appoints a leader (*raees shora-e enkeshafi*), an official position recognized by the government. The position of CDC head may or may not be influential, depending on the individual occupying the post. Many times a community leader, such as a malik or zamindar, will be appointed to this post, in which case the position allows him to consolidate his influence.

Municipalities are governance structures that work independently from provincial and district governance. The municipality of Farah is led by a mayor who is appointed by the president in consultation with the governor. Municipalities and the mayors who run them do not come under the formal control of the provincial governor. Municipalities are required by law to raise revenue from local sources and sustain their operations and services entirely out of such revenues.

HOW IT ACTUALLY WORKS

Governance in Farah remains unstable due to insecurity, criminal activity (particularly kidnapping), the weak capacity of the state, lack of development activities in the districts, and drug trafficking. The new provincial administration of Governor Rohul Amin appears relatively efficient and is in good standing with the people. The new administration and the governor have made progress on a number of fronts, including political outreach to the Provincial Council (PC) and community elders who play an important role in Afghanistan's traditional tribal society. Because government control is limited in most of the districts and the traditional local shuras are under pressure and threat from insurgents, Farah authorities face an uphill battle to strengthen provincial-district relationships.

In 2008 the central government made a number of key personnel and policy changes to Farah's security organizations. Of note, ISAF troops trained police officers in how to apply "escalation of force" procedures to protect the public. Many of the new personnel have previously fought against or were imprisoned by the Taliban, so they are motivated beyond just earning a paycheck. As of 2010 the new security leadership and the governor's administration have started to curtail crime rates, particularly abduction. They also claim to have countered a rising insurgency in several volatile districts, including Bakwa, Gulistan, Pur Chaman, and Bala Baluk.

In order to rebuild Alizai Pasthun confidence in Bala Baluk's district capital of Shiwan, the central government appointed General Faqir Askar as the new chief of police. He replaced Colonel Ghafar Khan, who was not effective and did not visibly counter the insurgent or illicit drug activity in the district. Immediately after his appointment, General Faqir Askar made several visits to Alizai elders in Shiwan aimed at encouraging them to join the government and benefit from development and other assistance from the government and aid groups. This engagement helped to rebuild local Alizai trust in the government.

The provincial chief of the NDS is concerned that the efforts to strengthen relations with Alizai in Shiwan will attract the Taliban, who have been known to recruit from those tribes it sees as influential or key to a particular area. This strategy allows them to more easily penetrate the districts they are trying to turn. Furthermore, reliable sources allege that police leadership has set up illegal checkpoints along the border, where the income is particularly high due to illicit activity. Similar checkpoints exist throughout Farah, but primarily in those areas with truck and convoy traffic.

Village Governance

In the rural areas, Afghan villages are defined less by their geographic boundaries and more by a strong sense of community and belonging. Rural villages are essentially clusters of independent families. The village may go by different names depending upon whom one asks. It may be named after someone significant in the village, in which case the name may be changed when that person dies. Villages often have minimal government presence.

There are five types of Afghan village leadership and supporting leadership positions: political, economic, religious, tribal, and military. Not every village will have each type of leader, and there may be more than one leader in each category. Some terms such as malik and khan are used generically to mean "leader" and can cause confusion.

Political Leadership: The *malik* is the village representative to the state. He will interact with district and provincial officials and officials from international NGOs or coalition forces. A malik is often elected or appointed by villagers, who pay him for his services.

Economic Leadership: In an agricultural community, the *arbabs, zamindars,* or *khans* are the landholders or landlords. These positions are found more often in southern Afghanistan, where larger land-holdings are common. These landlords are the chief employers and drivers of the village's economy. In addition to providing the economic backbone of the village, the economic leader also provides some basic community services, such as a salary for the village mullah, following customary cultural guidelines of generosity.

Religious Leadership: Each village will probably have at least one mullah. Village mullahs play an extremely important role in the community—they preside at births, weddings, deaths, and other significant societal events. Depending on the size or isolation of the village, a mullah may also be the only teacher, dispenser of folk medicine, or legal authority. Different ethnic or tribal cliques (qawms) may opt to have their own mullahs.

Tribal Leadership: The true tribal leader, known as the *khan* or *mesher*, is not generally considered part of the village leadership, as his focus is more on the function of the tribe. His sphere of influence may encompass several villages. But the tribal leader does have influence on his tribe's activities in a village. If a tribal leader does reside in a particular village, his responsibility and influence will certainly extend beyond it.

The tribal leader is not the same as one of the local village elders (see below), although he most likely engages with the local elders in order to understand the local situation. The collective tribal, clan, or village leadership institutions—the jirga or shura—connect the local village leaders with the larger tribal qawm led by the tribal leader.

The position of tribal leader may or may not be a powerful one, depending on the cohesiveness of the tribe, its size, its wealth, the personality of the tribal leader, and other factors.

Military Leadership: Some villages may have a military commander, known as the *qomandan* or *komandan*. This commander may have variable prominence within the village hierarchy. A powerful qomandan may become a local warlord. Following the anti-Soviet jihad, qomandans and their desire to gain more power and revenue was one factor that led to the Afghan civil war. This recent memory is one reason why a strong or permanent military commander may not be welcomed by all residents and current power holders.

Supporting Leadership Roles

Other additional positions may have a degree of power or influence depending on local situations. Supporting leadership roles in villages vary region to region and village to village. The following list of known supporting roles is not exhaustive, but it indicates what each position involves.

Mohasen or rish safid (village elders) are the "white beard" or "grey beard" men of the village who offer their wisdom in collective jirgas or shuras and mediate conflicts between other village leaders and powerbrokers. Their authority is not formal, but their power comes from their ability to influence other powerbrokers.

The **mirab (village water manager)** manages the village water supply, resolves disputes about water resources, and helps plan the agricultural economy of the village.

Appointed by the zamindar, the **chak bashi (village agricultural specialist)** works closely with farmers to coordinate agricultural activities in the area.

Other villagers may have some unofficial status as leaders, due to their professions (teachers or doctors), education, or perceived worldliness. Villagers may have these people engage with outsiders, but they are probably not the key leaders or decision makers themselves.

Titles of respect are abundant in Afghanistan. Engineer, Maulawi, Haji, and Sayed are all titles of respect that many people will place in front of their names. These titles are not reserved for people who are leaders or experts. They are honorific titles. As a sign of respect to the title holder, people may often defer to those with titles during discussions. Engineer is a title granted to people who have received an engineering degree, Maulawi is given to Sunni Muslim scholars,

Haji is reserved for those who have completed the *Haj* (pilgrimage) to Mecca, and Sayed is reserved for men who are recognized as being descendents of the Prophet Muhammad.

SECURITY FORCES

Afghan National Police (ANP)

The local population believes that the ANP is abusing its government backed authority by performing illegal searches, unnecessarily harassing the public, extorting bribes or "protection money," and otherwise abusing their power. In April 2008 three senior officials within the Farah ANP—the director of intelligence, the chief of counter-narcotics, and the head of the terrorism department—were suspected of links with criminals and drug traffickers and were removed. Their replacements were new officers, most of whom came from outside the province. Despite initial hopes of positive changes after the reshuffle, improvement is needed, notably in districts affected by the insurgency (Bakwa, Gulistan, Khak-e Safid, and Bala Baluk).

Farah's provincial police force is still institutionally weak. It lacks sufficient manpower, training, equipment, and other logistical support. Thin police presence and corruption have made it easier for the Taliban and other groups to consolidate and spread their influence. Crime is also a major problem. Police trained through the Focused District Development (FDD) program have been vacating their posts in Bakwa, Bala Baluk, and Gulistan due to increased insecurity. Senior officers say it is difficult to convince these policemen to serve in such areas without providing more incentives. Nevertheless, the Ministry of the Interior is training and deploying 700 new recruits to districts of concern.

Afghan National Army (ANA)

In response to increased armed robberies along the Ring Road and repeated complaints by locals, the ANA 207 Corps has recently deployed additional troops to improve security. The ANA contingent is led by Lt. Col. Naimat Tajik from Kabul, who is not affiliated with any political party and is loyal to the government. He also enjoys local support for his positive performance. The ANP, ANA, and ISAF have conducted successful joint military operations in Bala Buluk, Gulistan, Bakwa, Khak-e Safid, and Farah Rod. In November 2009 the US Army built a large ANA brigade facility with modern equipment and facilities. The base accommodates more than 2,000 soldiers and includes a helicopter landing pad and a training ground for new recruits.

Afghan Border Police (ABP)

The border police for Farah province seem to regulate the flow of arms or smuggled goods rather than perform a formal customs role. The patrol reports illegal persons from Baluchistan and Iran, prevents people from crossing the border without required documents from Iran, and maintains a list of those persons it has allowed to come over the border. At times this information has been used to detain individuals in Farah and led to follow-up arrests. The Border Police are often seen as complicit in the bribery and corruption that pervade the country. Results of this corruption are evident in the poppy industry, trafficking in small arms, and movement of illegal persons between the countries. When it is in the ABP's interest to do so, it informs ISAF of small arms shipments or Iranian-trained Taliban coming across the border.

Table 4: Political Parties

Party	Leader	Description
Afghan Mellat (Afghan Nation)	Anwar al-Haq Ahadi	A Pashtun nationalist party that is very powerful throughout Afghanistan. Its members supported Karzai during the 2009 election.
Da Soley Ghorzan (Peace Movement)	Shahnawaz Tanai	Closely associated with one of Afghanistan's communist parties, its leader was the Defense Minister in Najibullah's government.
Freedom and Democracy Movement	Jawed Kohistani	A populist party calling for political reform, it has a close relationship with Jamiat-e Islami, but remains independent.
National Unity Party	Nur al-Haq Ulumi	A populist, left-leaning party originating in 1986.
Harakat-e Islami (IMA)	Mohammad Asef Mohseni	Founded along Shia principles, this party is popular among Hazaras but refused to join the Hazara coalition during the civil war.
Jamiat-e Islami Afghanistan (Islamic Society of Afghanistan)	Burhanuddin Rabbani	One of the original Islamist parties in Afghanistan, Jamiat-e Islami was established in the 1970s in Kabul University. Predominantly Tajik, the party fought the Soviet occupation and was a major force in the Northern Alliance. The most influential member within the party was Ahmad Shah Massoud, who led the military wing of Jamiat-e Islami throughout the 1980s.
Mahaz-e Milli Islami (National Islamic Front)	Pir Ishaq Gailani	Predominantly Pashtun, Mahaz-e Milli promotes national unity and is influential among some Sufis. Its founder and leader, Pir Ishaq Gailani, is also seen as the leader of the Qadiriyah sect of Sufism. Mahaz-e Milli has a reputation for moderate thought and the traditional, mystical, and introspective tenets that characterize Sufism.

POLITICAL PARTIES

Since the departure of the Taliban, Farah and its neighboring provinces have redefined many of their political parties. Women are now allowed to run for office and are commonly seen on voting posters with their face uncovered. Eight political parties are important in Farah. Of these, Afghan Mellat and the National Solidarity Movement hold the most influence.

Due to recent history, the political divide in Farah is between right wing jihadi commanders from Hezb-e Islami, Jamiat-e Islami, and Mahaz-e Melli and several former leftists (former Khalqis and Parchamis). In addition, a few relatively moderate and democratic parties are active in the province. One of them, the Afghan Mellat (Afghan Nation), has considerable influence among Pashtuns. From 2004 to 2008, the competition between the jihadis and leftists ensured that power in the provincial government was not monopolized by one specific group. Their influence waned after the central government began appointing key officials from outside the province in 2008. A list of political parties can be seen in Table 4.

LEADER PROFILES

Government and Political Leaders

Rohul Amin, Governor: Amin was a member of the Pakistan-Afghanistan Peace Jirga and was the director of WADAN, an NGO working in the field of peace, democracy, and development when it won the National Endowment for Democracy award in 2005. He was also a candidate in the 2005 parliamentary election. Governor Amin is affiliated with the Afghan Mellat (Afghan Nation) party, which is influential in the province, especially among Pashtuns. Initially seen as partial towards the Pashtuns, the governor has lately been praised by the people of the province for his political outreach, improvement of relations with the provincial council, shuras, and elders, and for directing security agencies to control criminal activities.

It is said that he is more western and less traditional in his approach. According to UNAMA observation, he has performed well, bringing positive changes to the local government and building unique relations with UNAMA, the PRT, DoS, USAID, and USDA. He has a positive reputation in the province and remains free of any allegations of corruption. His family lives in the US.

Faqir Mohammad Askar, Chief of Police: Askar was appointed Chief of Police in July 2009, replacing Abdul Ghafar. He is a university graduate and is a professional police officer. He is believed to have appointed his friends to high-paid positions in border areas where the drug mafia is active.

Colonel Samad Khan, NDS Chief: Colonel Khan is originally from Farah province and has served as Deputy NDS Chief in Zabul and Nimroz provinces for over three years. Samad Khan has a good understanding of the political and security situation in Farah and knows influential leaders and local insurgent groups active in the province. He maintains good relations with members of local government, in particular the Provincial Council and local shura in Farah City.

Nazir Khidmat, PC Chair: Nazir Khidmat was elected the new PC chair in March 2009, replacing Ms. Belqais Roshan. Khidmat is an ethnic Pashtun and a former member of ROWA in Pakistan. He is now a member of the Afghan Mellat party.

Malalai Joya: A former Member of Parliament for Farah, Malalai Joya gained international recognition as a female leader in Afghanistan for her stark criticism of the Karzai administration and her opposition to religious leaders holding prominent and influential government positions. In 2007 Democracy Now named her the "Bravest Woman in Afghanistan." She was suspended from Parliament by her fellow representatives because they believed she insulted several Members of Parliament during a television interview by calling them warlords. She remains very popular in the province and her suspension is under review.

Insurgent & Criminal Elements

Mullah Zaqir: Mullah Zaqir is perhaps the deadliest and most active Taliban commander in Farah since 2001. Following the death of Mullah Rashid in the spring of 2010, Mullah Zaqir united the Taliban factions in Farah and is seen as the current shadow governor of the province. His predecessors often coordinated and executed well thought out campaigns against GIRoA and ISAF troops. By contrast, Mullah Zaqir executes spontaneous attacks and is seen as unpredictable. He is known for kidnapping government officials, teachers, public servants, and policemen, often beheading them without thought.

An Achakzai from the Zirak branch of the Durrani super-tribe, Mullah Zaqir is thought to be in his mid-20s. Originally from Range village in Khak-e Safid, his area of operations changes but he often operates in Pusht Rod and Bala Baluk. He is widely known to be illiterate and got his start as a gang leader. He executes mandates from the Taliban's Quetta Shura and receives direct support from them in the form of suicide bombers, vests, remote control equipment, and other devices used to further his campaign. He will often hold meetings with his Taliban counterparts to identify assassination targets. Under his leadership, there is minimal infighting between Taliban leaders in Farah.

Mullah Baz Muhammad: Mullah Baz Muhammad is a Taliban leader based in Pusht Rod just north of Masow and Chien Farsi. He came to prominence during the Taliban era, serving as the district sub-governor of Shindand district in Herat. In this position he was known to be more sympathetic to the people, listening to their needs and

The security situation in Farah has deteriorated over the past few years. Locals have grown distrustful of government officials and police, as well as foreign armies and workers. The government has begun to focus on better training for their officers, but many new trainees have deserted their post due to lack of support and poor pay.

PHOTO BY SENIOR AIRMAN RYLAN K. ALBRIGHT

trying to make their lives better. This approach has made him popular in Farah, where he currently acts as the local power broker in Pusht Rod.

A Noorzai, he has a strong relationship with Mullah Zaqir, and many people believe they are related even though they are from different tribes. Mullah Baz Muhammad is very protective of his community and does not permit criminal activity unless authorized by the Taliban leadership. People appreciate his concern and often bring him gifts and money as thanks. While he coordinates and supports other Taliban elements in the area, he does not attack ISAF troops unless they interfere with his area of influence.

Mullah Abdul Manan: One of the Taliban's top commanders for Farah province, Mullah Abdul Manan is a former Taliban-era district police chief. He has frequently led ambushes against ANSF and ISAF troops. He was previously held by the US military but released during a covert prisoner exchange between the Afghan government and insurgents who kidnapped two National Solidarity Program employees in September 2006. Manan re-established his role as an insurgent commander with support from the Taliban's top leadership and continues to lead deadly attacks in Bakwa and Bala Baluk districts.

Mullah Abdul Ghani: Ghani is a known weapons and explosives facilitator in Anar Dara district. In March 2003 coalition forces raided a compound he owned, where they seized weapons arriving from smugglers operating along the Iranian-Afghan border. The weapons shipment contained antipersonnel/antitank mines.

Mullah Rashid: Rashid is responsible for coordinating and consolidating insurgent groups in the region. His role includes distributing money collected from the mafia that smuggles narcotics in and out of Iran. He also distributes food, arms, and ammunition from international supporters. In May 2010 Rashid made a secret visit to Herat City to meet with former Taliban associates to gain their support to expand their activities in the region.

Agriculture is the largest sector of the economy in Farah. In September 2010 officials broke ground on a new Farah Wholesale Market to help farmers sell their produce. Most farmers live at a subsistence level, but the governor hopes that better markets will increase profits for farmers.

PHOTO BY SENIOR AIRMAN RYLAN K. ALBRIGHT

Chapter 4
The Economy

Farah's location between Kandahar and Herat was a key to its early growth. But when the Ring Road was completed in 1965, it bypassed Farah City and diminished the province's importance as a trading hub. Today the province's economy is based on subsistence agriculture. Most farmers get their irrigation from rivers or canals, but the province's water management infrastructure is in disrepair. A few people keep livestock, but it is not widespread enough to have a major impact on the economy. With the exception of Routes 1, 517, and 515, most roads in the province are in poor condition, making it difficult for people to move goods or crops to markets in Herat and Delaram. As a result, most licit trade from Iran comes through Nimroz and Herat provinces, not Farah. Narcotics smugglers do cross the border with Iran, but it is diffticult to determine how much of the province's economy is based on this trade.

INFRASTRUCTURE

Electricity

Farah's electricity infrastructure is poor compared to nearby Herat and Nimroz, which receive most of their electricity from Iran. Sections of Farah City receive electricity from five fuel-based power

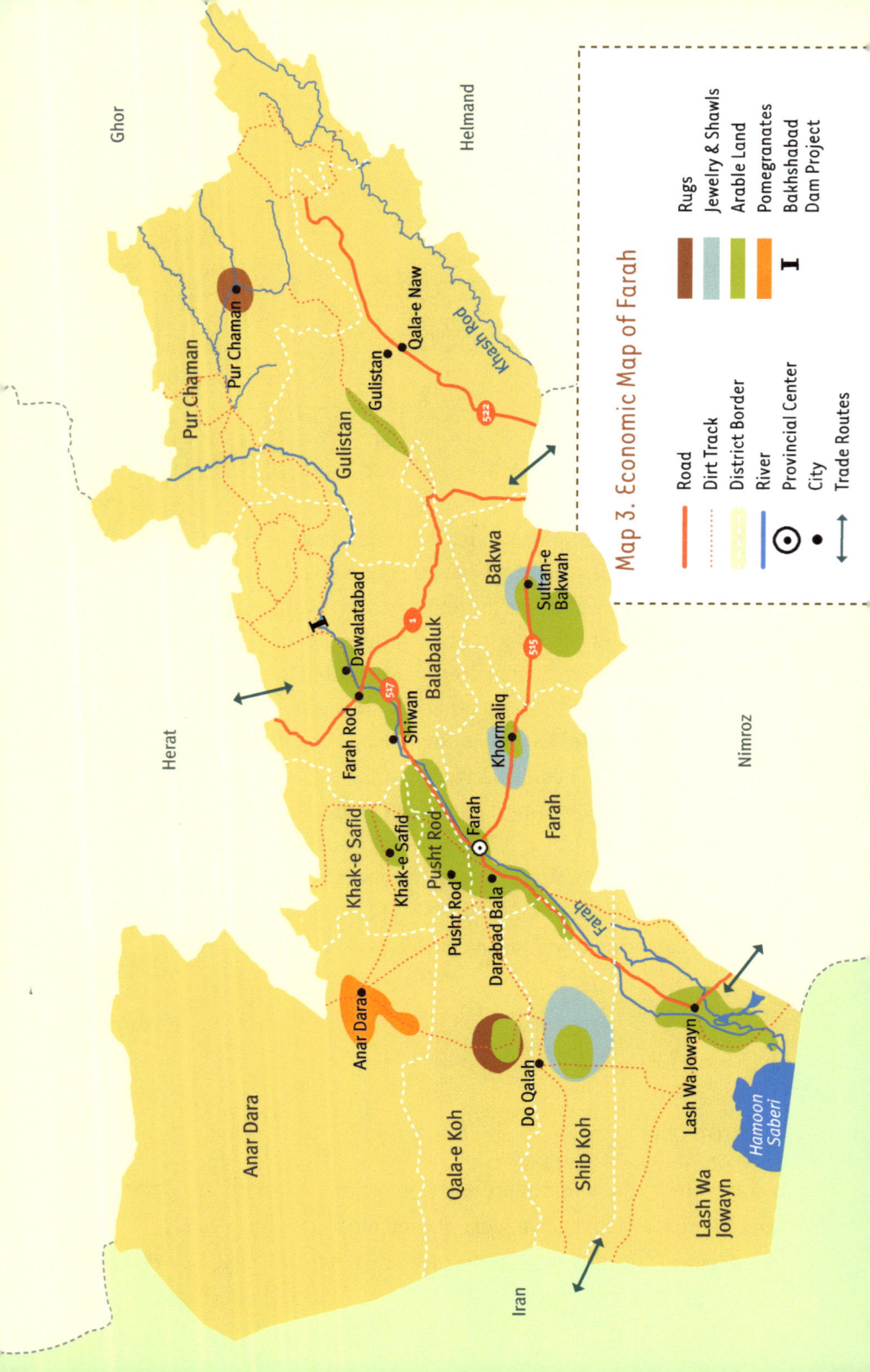

generators with a capacity of 1,190 kW for a few hours per day. The US PRT provides the fuel for some of these power generators. In some parts of the province, Farah City in particular, communities have taken the initiative to either hire or purchase power generators for themselves. Some households use solar panels to generate electricity, but it is not common in the province. Overall, an estimated nine percent of households in Farah have access to electricity, but with the growth of media and communication, the demand for electricity is rising. Natural gas is imported from Iran and Turkmenistan, with one private gas firm operating in Farah province. Fuel is also imported from Iran. There are four governmental and 36 private fuel stations operating in the province.

Transportation

Nearly half (49 percent) of the roads in the province are able to handle traffic in all seasons and about an additional third (34 percent) are able to handle traffic in some seasons. However, heavy sand storms often hinder travel between districts and the provincial center. Lash Wa Juwayn, in particular, is isolated from the rest of the province due to poor road conditions. The inhabitants of Khak-e Safid do not have a bridge connecting them to the provincial center. So they have to take a 50-kilometer, two-and-a-half hour detour.

Irrigation

Farah has 100,000 hectares of irrigated land. The Farah River serves as the major waterway for the province. The Khash Rod River, Nizgan River, and three major water canals provide irrigation to farmers. The Khash Rod River flows down the mountains, providing Gulistan district with a good source of irrigation. While no comprehensive water table or watershed studies have been conducted in the province, micro-hydrologists believe that a substantial water table exists beneath the district of Bala Baluk. With the assistance of various international aid organizations, a loose network of water cooperatives help determine how best to use the river water and deal with flood plains, natural and manmade dams, arguments over water diversion for irrigation, and the placement of gabions, culverts, and retaining walls. A complex and, in places, very old system of aqueducts and *karezes* (a system of underground canals) has been used for generations and make it difficult to evaluate a better water management system.

Communication

The Telecommunications Department of the Ministry of Communications and Information Technology actively operates in the province, and Afghan Telecom, AWCC, and Roshan are functional in Farah City and surrounding villages. Over 40 percent of the population has access to cell coverage in the province. Phone cards can be purchased in USD in increments of $1.00, $3.00, $5.00, $10.00, and $20.00. Farahis commonly carry more than one cell phone, each with different carriers. There is no cell phone coverage in Pur Chaman and Gulistan, so all communication must be performed by a satellite phone (Thuraya provides the coverage).

KEY ECONOMIC SECTORS

Agriculture

Agriculture is the main industry in Farah. There are a number of farmers' cooperatives, one fertilizer company, and two high schools devoted to agriculture and animal husbandry. Farah's primary agricultural products—wheat, poppy, barley, corn, onion, okra, almonds, and fruits such as grapes, pomegranates, apples, and pistachios—are sold in downtown markets of Herat, Nimroz, Helmand, Kandahar, and Kabul, and some are exported to Iran and Pakistan. Pomegranates are the major product of Anar Dara (the Pomegranate Valley) and poppy (opium) is usually grown in the insecure districts of Gulistan, Bala Baluk, Khak-e Safid, and Pusht Rod. In 2005, the last date for which Ministry statistics are available, five agricultural cooperatives were active in Farah. The 250-farmer-strong cooperative cultivated approximately 3,000 hectares of land and produced an average of over 1,000 tons of produce for sale. Each farmer held shares in the cooperative worth approximately 54,800 AFS ($1,212). Farmers continue to request that the government or aid agencies purchase subsidized surplus wheat in lean years in order to maintain the economic viability of licit crops.

Livestock

Farah is largely an agrarian community and does not rely heavily on livestock. There are not many butcheries or ranches in the province. In outlying districts, livestock is limited to small goats and occasional flocks of sheep, which are often limited to less than 25 animals per flock. Still, local wool, meat, milk, and dairy products can be found at bazaars. Wool is often taken from available livestock and sold in the markets to be used to weave rugs, carpets, and other locally worn

A man works in the greenhouse at Farah City Agricultural School. Wheat and fruits are cultivated at the school, though lengthy droughts and a lack of irrigation mean that poppies are commonly grown in rural areas.

PHOTO BY SENIOR AIRMAN RYLAN K. ALBRIGHT

textiles. Kuchis also graze their livestock throughout the province, especially in the winter months. There are more than 400 poultry farms now in Farah.

Minor Industry

By and large small industry is absent in Farah with minor production of handicrafts related to carpets, rugs, jewelry, and shawls. Carpets and tapestry-woven rugs are mainly produced in Qala-e Kah and Pur Chaman, and jewelry and shawls are produced in Farah, Pusht Rod, Shib Koh, and Bakwa districts.

Trade and Finance

Da Afghanistan Bank has one branch in the province. Farah has one main customs house in the provincial capital and five branches along the border with Iran. Despite the recent bank crisis, the province's Finance Department believes that two private banks—Kabul Bank and Azizi Bank—are operating now in Farah. A 2005 Department of Economy report claimed that 37 percent of households in Farah had taken out loans, and 19 percent were invested in economic activity, such as small loans to farmers to purchase more livestock from neighbors, land, water usage, milk, or wool to trade in and out of the market.

Farah's primary trade routes are via Delaram to the south, Herat to the north, and Iran to the west. Goods from Iran include finished and refined goods, such as machinery, tools, and electrical equipment. Supplies for vehicle maintenance and other necessary parts for industrial equipment also arrive from Iran. Candies, sweets, and popular sodas come from Iran and are stamped plainly on the side. Other products arriving from Iran include poultry and meat, which shores up the deficiency in available meat throughout the province.

Provincial Reconstruction Team engineers and civil affairs members move along the Kineske Canal with a member of the Kineske Council. A number of cash-for-work projects have been implemented in the province to clean and expand canals. By improving the irrigation system, farmers hope to be able to grow crops in more than one season.

PHOTO BY SENIOR AIRMAN RYLAN K. ALBRIGHT

Chapter 5
International Community and Reconstruction Activities

PROVINCIAL RECONSTRUCTION TEAM (PRT)

ISAF operations in Farah fall under the command of Regional Command (RC) West. The PRT in Farah was officially founded September 15, 2005. The PRT is a joint, integrated military-civilian organization designed to improve security, extend the political reach of the Afghan government, and facilitate reconstruction and development throughout the province. Because of the combined capabilities of its diplomacy, defense, and development components, the integrated nature of the PRT allows it to penetrate and stabilize the more unstable and insecure areas of a province. The military side consists of a Civil Affairs (CA), Public Affairs, and Engineering Teams, plus support elements. The civilian side consists of representatives from the US Agency for International Development (USAID), US Department of State (DoS), and US Department of Agriculture (USDA). A new addition to the PRT is the Agribusiness Development Team (ADT), consisting of National Guard soldiers with several agriculture specialties. The ADT is co-located on-board the PRT. They retain administrative control of their personnel but share operational control with the PRT and its commander.

The PRT seeks to connect the people of Farah to the government through engagement and mentoring. Using Commander's Emergency Response Program (CERP) funding, the PRT contributed more than $8 million USD to the development of Farah during 2009 and into 2010. The projects primarily focused on infrastructure for the province in sanitation, water, hard structures, agriculture, roads, and medical facilities. Key projects of note are the provision of electricity to Farah Hospital, the construction of Route 515, the clearing of the Khak-e Safid Canal, and the completion of the surveys necessary to reinvigorate the Bakshabad Dam reconstruction effort. As of October 2010, the dam project was not funded.

The Ministry of Energy and Water's Department of Water Management works alongside the Department of Rural Rehabilitation and Development to identify key river networks that impact local communities and how they can best take advantage of their natural location without disrupting communities who live downstream. For this reason many implementers working for USAID require a waiver should they identify key irrigation projects requested by the Department of Water Management or Ministry of Rural Rehabilitation and Development.

NATIONAL SOLIDARITY PROGRAM (NSP)

The National Solidarity Program (NSP) helps develop the ability of Afghan communities to identify, plan, manage and monitor their own development projects. The program is active in six districts in Farah: Farah, Pusht Rod, Bala Baluk, Bakwa, Lash Wa Juwayn, and Anar Dara. NSP works through Community Development Councils (CDCs) and submits its proposals through the District Development Assembly (DDA). About 1,040 NSP projects, worth a total of $16.5 million, were executed between 2007 and 2010. Projects included the construction of roads, culverts, irrigation canals, drinking water wells, schools, and the construction and cleaning of *karezes*. The NSP program is implemented nationally through the Ministry of Rural Rehabilitation and Development (MRRD), primarily with World Bank funding.

PROJECTS AND ACTIVITIES

Institutional Development and Governance

The main challenges to development in the province include insurgent activities, limited government capacity, low presence of the international community and local donors, and little support from the central government. While these factors have had a negative impact, sub-national governance has made some gains since the appointment of Farah City Mayor Abdul Rahim Isakzai in May 2008. He has been actively engaged in implementing five developmental goals: constructing roads, creating a clean water supply system, bringing electricity to the city, providing a home for refugees, and cleaning up Farah City.

The Public Administration Reform/Priority Reform and Restructuring (PAR/PRR) process in Farah has not helped developmental progress due to a significant shortage of resources and reluctance toward change by the former provincial leadership. There was little progress in implementing planned civil service reforms that require filling the positions of grade six to ten (at the provincial level) based on merit appointments.

USAID's Local Governance and Community Development (LGCD) program started in Farah in mid-2008. The local governance component of the program approved building of a multi-purpose training center and several new district centers. Farah, much like its neighboring provinces, has a Provincial Development Committee (PDC) responsible for organizing, deconflicting, prioritizing, unifying, and approving development efforts province wide. However, deficient training, lack of leadership, disparate political interests, and tribal differences have undermined the PDC's capabilities. Farah, one of the volatile provinces, was targeted under the Phase II roll out in August 2008 for the establishment of a Provincial Management Unit (PMU), which is designed to manage operations at the provincial level under the overall coordination of the PDC. The governor committed himself to run the Afghanistan Social Outreach Program (ASOP), started by the national Independent Directorate of Local Governance in 2008 to support traditional governance structures, such as the tribal shura, with formal governance structures. ASOP is widely supported by the international community and funded through donors, including USAID. Currently ASOP is in its preparatory phase (collection of accurate and reliable data on existing security trends, governance structures, and development interventions).

Humanitarian

The humanitarian challenges in the province include droughts, seasonal sandstorms, forced and voluntary migration across the Iranian border, disease outbreaks, and consequences of insurgent activity. The Provincial Disaster Management Committee (PDMC), led by the governor, is functioning as a coordination cell but still requires significant support from NGOs, ISAF and the donor community to plan and execute response to natural disasters. During the winter of 2010-2011, 2,000 packages of relief items were pre-positioned in Farah to enable the provincial PDMC to respond to any likely winter crises. Of the 2,000 non-food packages pre-positioned by UNHCR and UNICEF, 1,800 packages were distributed to the winter-exposed and/or affected families before the heavy winter storms.

The governmental departments have very limited capacity to deliver assistance effectively. The international community has encountered several problems when dealing with the provincial authorities, including a lack of accurate and timely reporting, limited accountability, little coherence and follow up, lack of commitment, and lack of coordination among the government line departments.

Limited rainfall this year in Farah suggests the recurrence of drought in the province again in 2010. Only two cubic inches of rain has fallen in Farah since the beginning of winter (about five cubic inches is normal).

Refugees

In addition to people suffering from environmental hardships, Farah's Director of Refugees and Repatriation (DoRR) estimates that four million Afghan refugees live in Iran, some illegally. Many of these refugees emigrated to Iran for better economic opportunities or to work as temporary laborers. About 90 percent of the men in Farah work as laborers in Iran at some point in their lives, many illegally. About 6,500 refugee families have returned from Iran to Farah to date. Approximately 80 percent of those, or 5,200 families, have remained in the province. About 200 families currently live in a refugee settlement for internally displaced persons (IDPs) within a few kilometers of the PRT. The DoRR plans to expand it to house 6,000 families. Other families could settle in the desert if shelter and water were provided.

Iran deports many Farahi en masse every year. The mass deportations primarily occur in the winter and involve upward of 1,000 people of all ages and genders. Carried by large trucks and dropped at the border, they are not brought to any district center or released in the vicinity of any other populated area. Though exact figures do not exist, reports suggest that a large number of infants and elderly perish from the severe winter climate.

In terms of assistance, the World Food Program has provided food packets for 2,000 families and the International Organization of Migration (IOM) has provided 1,000 shelters and assistance to about 3,500 families, according to the DoRR. The greater concern is that the DoRR does not have a systematic plan to deal with the situation, other than hoping the NGOs will take care of the problem. Returnees place an additional burden on the economy, increase competition for jobs, and become targets for insurgent recruitment. Successful governance in the border provinces requires that local authorities plan for the integration or relocation of IDPs.

Electricity

The Bakhshabad Dam project and alternative sources of clean energy are the only projects that focus on electricity in the province. The dam is expected to generate 20 to 40 MW of electricity, but Iran has objected to the dam's construction because it would decrease the water it receives from the Farah River. Among the alternative energy projects are proposals to install solar panels in the district governors' compounds in Pusht Rod and Bala Baluk.

Transportation

A 75-kilometer paved road connecting Farah City and Farah Rod was completed in 2010 after three years of work. Similarly the 23-kilometer road connecting Farah City to Khormaliq and the 68-kilometer road leading from Farah to Route 1 (Ring Road) were paved in 2010. These road projects helped farmers gain access to new markets. The PRT is also planning to build a road between Chien Farsi and Masow, two important villages in Pusht Rod district.

Irrigation

Under USAID's Food Insecurity Response for Urban Population (FIRUP) program, the Central Asia Development Group runs several karez and canal cleaning and restoration programs. The budgets for these programs run between $5,000 and $25,000 each. In addition, cash-for-work programs under USAID's Alternative Development Program-Southwest (ADP/SW) have been used to repair and clean karezes and canals around the province. For example, the Tewask Canal Rehabilitation Project cleared the canal of vegetation and widened it for better water flow.

Healthcare

The healthcare facilities in Farah are largely inadequate for anything larger than minor injuries. The province has several clinics for basic vaccinations, bandaging, setting of broken bones, and necessary first aid. Most residents travel to Kabul for more urgent care. Dental facilities are also inadequate lacking local professionals and practitioners. Extracts of opium based products are available at local pharmacies as a quick solution for comfort or pain relief.

Farah's Department of Public Health continues to support improved access to clinical services, promote the development of human resources in the health sector to reduce disease, increase life expectancy, and promote the overall health and well-being of the population. There are ten health clinics and one hospital with a combined total of 60 beds. There are 42 pharmacies within Farah province, of which 40 are privately owned and two are government operated.

The outlying communities in districts surrounding Farah City largely lack access to healthcare. About 70 percent have access to a nearby Basic Health Care (BHC) facility, which lacks important equipment and beds. The BHC is a small facility that offers limited curative care, including diagnosis and treatment of malaria, diarrhea, and acute respiratory infection; distribution of condoms and oral contraceptives, and subsequent depot progesterone (DMPA) injections; and micronutrient supplementation. The BHC healthcare workers are responsible for treating illnesses and conditions common in children and adults. The services of the BHC will cover a population of 15,000 to 30,000, depending on the local geographic conditions and the population density. In circumstances where the population is very isolated, the minimum population for a BHC can be less than 15,000. The minimal staffing requirements for a BHC are a nurse, a community midwife, and two vaccinators.

Only about two percent of people have access to a health center and three percent have access to a dispensary within their village. Nearly three out of four people (73 percent) have to travel more than ten kilometers to reach their closest health facility.

Education

Farah's urban population believes that education will help reduce poverty and facilitate economic growth. The overall literacy rate in Farah province is 21 percent, with 27 percent of men and only 14 percent of women being literate. Thirty percent of men and 12 percent of women between the ages of 15 and 24 are literate. The Kuchi population in the province has significantly lower levels of literacy: less than four percent for men and less than one percent for women.

Table 5: USAID Projects

Name of Project	Implementing Partner	Focus of Project
Afghan Civilian Assistance Program (ACAP)	International Organization for Migration (IOM)	Afghan victims of war. The program assesses families in regards to combat damages and injury, and provides grants and assistance to help in the restoration of their livelihoods. This is often an under-utilized program because it takes time for the investigation of the incident and is not an immediate response for the affected families. Additionally, many incidents are simply not reported to the ACAP program for further investigation.
Alternative Development Program – Southwestern Region (ADP/SW)	Association for Rural Development, Inc. (ARD)	Implements alternative agricultural products.
Food Insecurity Response for Urban Populations (FIRUP)	Central Asian Development Group (CADG)	Cash for work on local infrastructure.
Assistance to the Civil Service Commission (ACSC)	Deloitte	Trains Afghan civil servants to improve the delivery of government services at the national and sub-national level.
The Ambassador's Small Grant's Program (ASGP)	N/A	Flexible grants for capacity building address Afghan women's needs in education, healthcare, economic opportunity, family counseling, and public advocacy.
Education Quality Improvement Program (EQUIP)	UN-Habitat	Supports education activities.

Overall, there are 238 primary and secondary schools in Farah. About 32 percent of all children, or 99,172, between six and 13 are enrolled in school (37 percent of boys and 26 percent of girls). Boys account for 70 percent of students, and 84 percent of the schools are boys' schools. Because Kuchis are nomadic, only four percent of boys and one percent of girls from these communities attend school in Farah during the winter and summer months. There are 2,542 teachers working in schools in Farah province, one fifth (21 percent) of whom are women.

INTERNATIONAL ORGANIZATIONS AND THE UNITED NATIONS

In July 2006 a team of facilitators from the National Area-Based Development Program (NABDP) of the MRRD travelled to Farah City to facilitate a community-led comprehensive development planning process. With the support of the NABDP facilitators, the District Development Assembly (DDA) and district government representatives drafted a District Development Plan (DDP). The DDP enabled the communities to articulate their priority needs and recommend strategies for addressing them. The Provincial Reconstruction Team (PRT), US Agency for International Development (USAID), United Nations (UN) and GIRoA's Ministry of Rural Rehabilitation and Development (MRRD) are the primary supporters of construction, stabilization, and development projects in the province. The United Nations Assistance Mission in Afghanistan (UNAMA) established its office in the early part of 2010 to support the local government and to coordinate GIRoA and donor assistance efforts.

In late 2010 President Karzai announced that private security firms would be banned from working in Afghanistan. The ban, which goes into effect in February 2011, would forbid development firms and non-governmental organizations to employ private security guards to protect their personnel or projects. An estimated $1.4 billion of development projects risk being shut down.

Table 6: Other Development Activities

Actor	Projects	Districts
UNICEF	Water Supply and Sanitation	Farah, Anar Dara, Bala Baluk
	Health	Pusht Rod, Lash Wa Juwayn, Bakwa
	Education	Farah, Anar Dara, Pusht Rod, Lash Wa Juwayn, Bala Baluk, Bakwa
UNHCR	Shelter and Winterization	Farah, Anar Dara, Pusht Rod, Lash Wa Juwayn, Bala Baluk
	Income Generation	Farah, Bala Baluk
	Water	Farah, Anar Dara, Bala Baluk
UNAMA	Election Coordination	Farah, Bala Baluk
UNOPS	Water, Sanitation, Road Access, Culverts, Agriculture, and Election (CDP: Program for Disabled People)	Farah, Bala Baluk
UNFAO	Agriculture, Animal Husbandry Clinic, and Chicken Hatcheries	Farah, Bala Baluk
UN-Habitat	Culvert and Gravelling	Farah, Bala Baluk
	City Canal Construction, NSP	Farah
	School Construction, Wells	Bala Baluk
WHO	Vaccination Program	Farah, Bala Baluk
	Health	Lash Wa Juwayn
IOM	Clinic Construction, School Rehabilitation/Reconstruction	Farah, Anar Dara
	Women Department	Farah
	School Construction, Road Rehabilitation, and Karez Cleaning	Lash Wa Juwayn
WFP	Food for Education and Food for Work	Farah, Lash Wa Juwayn, Bala Baluk
	Food Distribution	Pusht Rod
DACAAR	Water Supply	Farah, Anar Dara, Pusht Rod, Lash Wa Juwayn, Bala Baluk
HELP	School Construction and Support for Prisoner	Farah, Anar Dara
	Culvert and Karez Cleaning	Farah, Anar Dara, Pusht Rod
	Dams	Pusht Rod
OI	Shelter, Agriculture, Nursery, and Fertilizer	Farah
	Karez Digging, Fertilizer Distribution and Seeds Distribution	Pusht Rod
ALISIE	Karez Cleaning, Clinic Construction, and Wells	Farah

Actor	Projects	Districts
ICRC	Supports the local hospital/clinic and community services	Farah
WVI	Karez Cleaning	Farah
Asia Foundation	Performance Management Planning	Farah
CHA	Health	Farah, Anar Dara, Pusht Rod, Bala Baluk
	Road Construction, Agriculture, and Karez Cleaning	Farah, Anar Dara, Bala Baluk
	Road Graveling	Lash Wa Juwayn
	Culverts and Wells	Farah, Anar Dara, Lash Wa Juwayn, Bala Baluk
VARA	Culverts, and School Rehabilitation	Farah
	Road Gravelling	Farah, Bala Baluk
SWRCA	Income Generation, Karez Cleaning, Community Services, Winterization, and ARM	Farah
ADA	Agriculture, Irrigation, Livestock and Education	Farah, Pusht Rod, Bala Baluk
ARCS	Basic life support to clinics and first aid	Farah, Bala Baluk
CRDSA	Local governmental capacity building	Farah, Pusht Rod
HOLD	Local governmental capacity building	Farah
HDCAW	Women's education, human rights, and promotion of democracy	Farah
MSDO	Road Rehabilitation/Construction, Wells, and Culverts	Farah
SRO	Road Gravelling, Culvert, and Wells	Farah
RDR	School Construction, Road Graveling	Lash Wa Juwayn
ADA	Home-Based School, Teacher Training, and Agriculture	Farah, Bala Baluk
	Karez Cleaning	Farah
	Karez Digging, Education, Fertilizer and Seeds Distribution	Pusht Rod
NSP	Road Rehabilitation, Wells, School Construction, Electricity Supply, and Culverts	Farah, Pusht Rod, Bala Baluk, Bakwa, Lash Wa Juwayn, and Anar Dara

The province's low literacy rates prevent print media from having a sizable impact. Most information is disseminated by word of mouth or through the radio. Friday sermons at mosques are one of the most powerful ways to disseminate information. People will often learn of events from public announcements or by talking with their friends over a cup of tea.

PHOTO BY MASTER SGT. TRACY DEMARCO

Chapter 6
Information and Influence

Despite the arrival of modern technology in Farah, traditional networks of communication are still used throughout the province. While satellite (Thuraya) and cellular phone systems are available to those who can afford them, information is still transmitted more quickly in person via word of mouth. This verbal information distribution in communities with low literacy rates can become dangerous when groups or individuals deliberately pass along erroneous information to suit their own agendas, and communities are not able to check that information through written sources. The degree to which locals share news with outsiders—Taliban, coalition forces, international aid organizations, Afghan NGOs, and appointed government officials—depends on several factors: the audience, where the outsiders come from, what the outsiders represent, and what the people of Farah believe the outsiders will do with this information. If locals feel that the spread of news could be traced back to themselves or their community, they will refuse to offer information or simply "talk around" questions.

Informal mechanisms of information sharing are still common in bazaars, markets, and other areas where people gather en masse. Often an area will be bustling with people who have no reason to move about other than simply belonging to the crowd. In this environment people swap stories, rumors, and news from outside the province and abroad. Additional information-sharing takes place over the customary sharing of tea. Often the table will be set with mixed fruits, dates, or nuts from the region, depending on the importance of the meeting or shura.

Media in Afghanistan since the fall of the Taliban in 2001 has shown remarkable growth and a large surge in popularity. Under the Taliban regime, there were no broadcasters in Afghanistan aside from the state-controlled national output. Music and even kite flying were banned. At the start of 2002 there was no mobile phone network at all. Now over 8 million Afghans have handsets. Television, radio, newspapers, and magazines have boomed. Mobile phone banking is even developing and has been used for the transfer of money and salaries, presenting an opportunity to avoid the Taliban highway tax-checkpoints. The success of the media sector seems to reflect growing optimism in Afghanistan. However, the media in Farah suffers from a lack of governmental support and the threat of reprisal for free expression of ideas from the Taliban.

TELECOMMUNICATIONS

The telecom companies operating in Farah are Afghan Telecom, Roshan, and Afghan Wireless. Afghan Telecom operates in all districts except Bakwa and Bala Baluk, where insurgents frequently attack communication facilities and towers. Etisalat and Ariba have begun service in Farah, and the Provincial Development Plan (PDP) has proposed the construction of 3,000 landlines. Afghan Wireless and Roshan Telecom offer an internet-capable network for mobile phones in the province. But there is no reliable data about the level of its usage in the population. Official figures show that 45 percent of the population is currently using the telecom services in the province, but considering the relative poverty and inaccessibility of electricity to power the phones, this estimate is rather high.

MEDIA

Radio is the principal news medium for the people of Farah. There are two FM radio stations in the province. One is the provincial state-run radio, which mostly broadcasts government-related programs and other entertainment programs. The other is Radio Nawa, which is based in Kabul and repeats its broadcast in Farah. The more popular Radio Nawa has captured the heart of the majority of citizens since it broadcasts primarily entertainment programs. A considerable number of people listen to the Iranian radio stations, particularly Radio Zahidan and Radio Tehran. In many parts of Farah a battery-powered radio or hand-crank is the only available source of news. The PRT has distributed hand-crank radios in many rural areas.

Since 2008 the PRT has run Sada-e Azadi ("Voice of Freedom") radio and newspaper. Programming includes public service announcements and educational stories in Dari and Pashto. Content, developed by the ministries, covers health, human rights, and legal issues. The public is generally receptive to coalition media sources but is also very aware of propaganda and its intent.

Television is not as popular as radio largely because television sets aremore expensive and require more electricity. Only one of the two state-run television stations, Afghanistan National Television, is active in Farah, airing from 6:00 pm to 11:00 pm. Programs focus on reports of government related plans. Voice of America's (VOA's) TV service Ashna broadcasts nationally on Radio Television Afghanistan (RTA), the other state-run station, from 6:00 pm to 7:00 pm in Dari and Pashto. It is also available in Herat, Nimroz, and Kandahar. The programming is popular in these neighboring provinces, and people travelling into Farah often will discuss what was seen on these broadcasts. The programming can occasionally be picked up in Gulistan and Bakwa district of Farah.

The growth of media in Farah seems to be confined to electronic media. Newspapers and magazines are scarce due to the lack of a printing infrastructure and the low literacy rate. Daily Anees, Hewad, Islah, Klid, and Mursal are the prominent daily newspapers in Farah. Jawanan, Uswah, Ammragan are monthly Farah periodicals. Sistan Monthly is a state-run magazine published by the Farah Department of Information and Culture. Pegah (Aurora) is a private monthly paper mostly focused on educational and cultural subjects. Jawanan-e Farah Monthly (Farah Youth Monthly) is fueled and published by the Farah youth association and focuses on issues important to the younger generation. Osveh Monthly is published by Tawhid Koranic Center and seeks to raise religious awareness among Farah's population.

Locals in Pur Chaman destroy a poppy field after agreeing to develop other crops like wheat. Farah is the third largest producer of poppy in Afghanistan. The government has started several programs to reduce poppy production with mixed results.

PHOTO BY SENIOR AIRMAN RYLAN K. ALBRIGHT

Chapter 7
Big Issues

NARCOTICS

An arid climate, porous border, and unstable security have made Farah a historically large producer of opium poppy. In 2008 Farah was Afghanistan's second largest poppy producing province. According to the Ministry of Rural Rehabilitation and Development (MRRD) reports, Farah has dropped to third as of September 2010, with approximately 12,000 hectares under cultivation. Still, due to unemployment and the history of drought, poppy remains the main source of income for many, particularly in Bakwa, Bala Baluk, Khak-e Safid, Gulistan, and Pusht Rod. Some local communities voluntarily stopped cultivating poppy when the government promised to deliver working alternative livelihoods.

Without international donor support, the government was unable to fund the program or access many of the crop fields. The deteriorated security situation made government officials wary of going to these key districts without military support for fear of capture and execution. As a result, some farmers have turned back to poppy production. In addition, the government's poppy eradication efforts have focused on small farmers because wealthy farmers have been able to bribe their way past the program's consideration. Both the failure to provide alternatives and the targeting of small farmers has made communities more distrustful of the government.

There is substantial poppy smuggling through Baluchistan with the tacit assistance of the Afghan Border Patrol agents, who collect bribes. The routes and schedules vary, and to placate the government, the criminal elements sometimes give up a shipment or divulge the location of a convoy. Divulging the location of a shipment demonstrates government efficacy and reduces pressure on the criminal element, while operationally it acts as a decoy while a large shipment of small-arms, narcotics, or human-trafficking takes place at another location.

Extensive agriculture programs—encouraging wheat production, cash-for-work programs, and road projects— that open market accessibility have helped to decrease poppy production in the province. For example, the Livelihood Program was a planning committee devoted to alternative agricultural crops. They provided courses and information dedicated toward changing crops. It was effective among smaller and poorer farmers but the larger plantations bought their way out of the program or found a waiver. The PRT is convinced that continued USAID agriculture-multiplier programs focusing on alternative crops and market accessibility are key to the development and security of the province.

TALIBAN INSURGENCY

The Taliban in Farah are not monolithic; there are many factions and groups vying for influence. The senior appointments in the Farah Taliban are heavily influenced by the Taliban military Shura based in Quetta, Pakistan. The Quetta Shura also provides financial and human resources, as well as logistical support to insurgents in Farah.

Corruption in the local administration, the lack of development activities, and the weak presence of the national government all aid the Taliban's efforts in Farah. Taliban influence from neighboring Helmand, Nimroz, and Herat is very strong and fuels the insurgency in Farah. Recently, operations by Afghan National Security Forces (ANSF) and ISAF in Helmand and Nimroz have pushed the Taliban into safe havens in Farah. Proximity to Iran has also fueled the insurgency; many Afghans believe the Taliban receive direct training from Iranian forces. Iranians have also been caught in Farah with false papers, though it is unclear what their intentions were.

The insurgency is fueled by religious and political ideology and a lack of economic opportunity. The ideologically driven fighters believe that a foreign force has occupied the country and that they are waging *jihad* to liberate their land. Beside the self-identified members of the Taliban, there are many fighters who share ties with the Taliban but do not consider themselves members. These fighters question the legitimacy of the Afghan government and the presence of foreign forces. Many of them will not be interested in development work or anything that might give the government or foreign forces further legitimacy.

Due to these factors, Farah has borne the brunt of the insurgency's southwestern expansion since it rebounded in 2006. Initially the Taliban launched attacks on Farah from their various strongholds in neighboring Helmand province. They have since established footholds inside Farah itself, where they can recruit, coordinate, and launch attacks. Over time, Farah has become the Taliban's epicenter for terrorist operations and is now critical to its western operations.

Bala Baluk district is a stronghold of the Taliban in western Farah province. Much insurgent activity was once planned and executed there. The Taliban have used madrassas to indoctrinate residents of Bala Baluk against the government and foreigners. Hoping to prevent insurgent activities, coalition and Afghan forces launched a military operation in Bakwa and Bala Baluk districts to rid the areas of the Taliban, and ANSF successfully captured the Taliban's Shiwan headquarters in October 2009. But the area has gradually returned to its former status as a safe haven for insurgents. The village is considered a transit hub for the Taliban and drug smugglers coming from the south and moving towards the borders with Iran and Herat. The Taliban have gained support in the area because their presence has allowed drugs and weapons trafficking to flourish with impunity, creating a culture of dependence among locals.

Despite various security crackdowns in Khak-e Safid and Bakwa districts, violence continued to flare throughout the province in May 2010. After the influx of Helmandi members, the Taliban has warned civil servants in Khak-e Safid to leave their posts. Attacks on the World Food Program and security contractors' convoys along the highway have become more regular, negatively impacting the delivery of UN programs to the most vulnerable populations. In particular, Bala Baluk, Bakwa, Delaram, Khak-e Safid, Gulistan, and Pusht Rod districts are known as areas with considerable Taliban support. Most of these districts lack sufficient police and other necessary support infrastructure. When not engaging in political violence, the Taliban themselves are also involved in drug trafficking and in criminal activities such as kidnapping and extortion. In the fall of 2010, districts where the Taliban were previously not active were becoming insecure due to weak and limited government control and lack of general development activities.

Efforts made by the national government and coalition forces to counter Taliban influence have been ineffective so far. This is compounded by a public distrust of Afghan security forces, which are often seen as corrupt. A major effort to address common concerns of extortion and insecurity on the highways has yet to bear fruit.

CRIMINAL ACTIVITY

The province of Farah faces serious crime issues amid the continuation of the lucrative drug trade in the province, which has been rising along with the insurgency. These criminals are distinct from the insurgency. Locals see them as rogue elements that operate without being restrained by tribal morals or the strict ethical codes of the Taliban. Motivated by personal gain, criminals use the general insecurity in Farah to kidnap for ransom and to trade drugs, both strong sources of revenue. They smuggle and produce drugs in Farah, although according to some government officials, not all of the drug trade is connected to criminal elements. Holding persons for ransom, sending death threat letters, and other forms of intimidation are also used to leverage money from the local population.

Criminals often kidnap people in groups and target convoys moving along the highways. They will let one person go as part of the negotiating process before holding out for the final ransom. Foreigners are rarely kidnapped because they travel in larger groups and when they are targeted, criminals are often confronted by military or security personnel. Foreigners who are apprehended will be held indefinitely. If the captive is a woman or member of the military, the criminal or insurgent elements will hold onto the individuals for a longer period of time unless the kidnappers are threatened, have to abandon their location, or need to make a statement. Those captives who are returned are often discovered dead by beheading or a cut throat on the outside of town or in a ditch.

Other criminal incidents arise from the desire to settle old scores. Many actors see the current conflict as an opportunity to settle old disputes by manipulating coalition forces and their firepower into exacting a private revenge, unrelated to the coalition mission. As a result, ISAF has at times mistakenly targeted individuals and communities that do not have strong ties to the insurgency. In turn, these individuals and groups have become alienated and disconnected from the Afghan government and the international community and have turned to the insurgency for protection and restoration of their honor.

The Taliban has been able to exploit these feuds in order to contribute to Farah's insecurity. They will offer support to one side or offer to arbitrate fairly between the parties, demonstrating greater ability to deliver justice than the current government. Feuding populations can at times be manipulated by the insurgency and at other times remain independent of and supersede the insurgency. The inter-tribal feuds are brought about by conflicts of interest, usually conflicts over land or water that take a tribal or sub-tribal dimension.

POLICE REFORM

The people of Farah are more concerned with the improper behavior of police than the danger posed by the insurgency in the province. The local population believes that the ANP is abusing its government backed authority by performing illegal searches, unnecessarily harassing the public, extorting bribes or "protection money," and otherwise abusing their power. By contrast, key local personalities such as government officials, power-brokers, and business leaders are seen by the population as posing the "least security concern."

To address this, the government started a Focused District Development (FDD) process for police in Farah in May 2008. ANP personnel from three districts (Gulistan, Bala Baluk, and Bakwa) completed two months of extensive training under the FDD program. But the program has been ineffective because of the high turnover rate in training agencies, trainees being embedded with local forces only for short durations, inadequate compensation, absence without leave, and graduation assignments that vary widely in terms of risk. Additionally the Taliban views this as a recruitment base or a source of informants.

RELATIONS WITH IRAN

Provincial officials allege that Iran has been arming insurgents and sending them through its borders into Farah to incite insecurity and chaos. For locals this perception is a logical conclusion drawn from the presence of US forces in Farah, the proximity of Iran to the province, and the tensions between the US and Iran. The ANP believes it foiled an attempt by Iran to establish an operations camp in a village called Zikin in Anar Dara with the support of insurgents. Reports from the ANP indicate Iran is still training and arming Afghan insurgents in the vicinity of Bala Baluk.

Iran is involved in a few rehabilitation projects, including supplying a very limited amount of electricity to the province and organizing a few cultural activities. Based on a 2006 agreement that it signed with the previous governor of Farah, Iran is funding a 120 km road from the Iranian border into Farah City, but only a small portion of it has been completed. The Iranian government has also built customs stations on both sides of the border, though there are about 12 smuggling routes used by drug cartels to cross the border. Many provincial residents go to Iran for seasonal and long-term employment. Governor Amin believes that Iran has an inconsistent policy towards Afghanistan. On one hand, the Iranians offer to help with roads and electricity, but on the other they are trying to discourage the Afghan government from building the Bakhshabad Dam, which will affect Iran's water flow from Afghanistan. They are arming insurgents to keep the coalition forces "busy."

Islam is an important influence in Afghan society and in Farah a mosque is often both a religious and social gathering place. People will pray five times a day and will often meet friends at the mosque to talk about events and exchange rumors.

PHOTO BY 2ND LT. CHRISTINE A. DARIUS

APPENDICES

TIMELINE OF EVENTS

November 5, 2005: Malalai Joya elected by Farah to Parliament as its youngest member.

November 22, 2006: Da Afghanistan Bank in Farah opened.

July 14, 2007: Taliban insurgents seize three key districts of Farah: Gulistan, Bakwa. and Khak-e Safid.

May 5, 2009: Over 120 innocent civilians were killed when US war planes bombed villages of Gerani and Gangabad in Bala Baluk districts. President Karzai conducts surprise visit afterward to inspect the damage and condemn the act.

October 7, 2010: Mullah Basir, the council leader of the shuras when called together, was killed by the insurgency in Shiwan, Bala Baluk.

October 10, 2010: A large operation conducted jointly by combined force of about 2,000 ISAF and ANA troops were engaged in clearing operations in the vicinity of Chien Farsi, Pusht Rod. The insurgent forces were driven east and northward to Bala Baluk and crossed the main river to the north. The main bridge in Bala Baluk was destroyed during these operations.

October 14, 2010: Insurgents destroy another bridge in Bala Baluk because it was built by the government.

COMMON COMPLIMENTS OF ISAF TROOPS IN FARAH

- The local population likes interacting with ISAF troops when they are dismounted. The children especially enjoy talking to foreigners because they are less suspicious of outsiders.

- The people of Farah have found that Westerners are friendly to them. Some are surprised because the local stereotype is that Westerners are crude and abrupt.

- Locals are pleased that international aid and relief agencies follow through on their plans and complete their projects. They are also happy international development agencies have been receptive to the population's ideas for programs.

COMMON COMPLAINTS OF ISAF TROOPS IN FARAH

- People in Farah City complain that ISAF troops will often test their heavy and light weapons while at the Farah airstrip. The noise scares children and livestock in the city.

- Farahi believe that the government embezzles the majority of the international donor funding. They do not feel that international donors give the same weight to their opinions as that of the government.

- The population complains that troops will drive down their roads, push locals off to the side, and park in the middle of the street.

A DAY IN THE LIFE OF A FARAHI

The first hint of daylight is typically seen around 4:30 am during the summer months and around 7:00 am during the winter. Unlike other areas of Afghanistan, mosques in Farah City do not have access to broadcasting equipment. One can only hear the call to prayer when outside. Many will bring their rugs to pray in the gardens or other common work. Sometimes people take turns and borrow the same rug while others sit aside and make small talk.

Around 1:00 pm people will sit down for lunch either at a table with knife and fork or cross-legged on a carpet in a small circle. Men and women eat separately and share their news, secrets, and gossip while they eat. The meals are fairly simple. Poultry, meats, and fish are found with the obvious exception of pork. The fish comes from Pakistan and Iran and is served in a herbal type of sauce over rice. The chicken is often served diced with a cream sauce and the beef is typically served on skewers like kabobs intermixed with tomatoes, green bell peppers, and onions. Salads are prepared with sliced cucumbers and tomatoes aligned in rows with a garnish of fruit in the middle and pistachios along the rim of the dish.

The men will always greet other men with a warm handshake and an earnest desire to make a strong first impression. They are polite to a fault. When entering or departing a doorway they will always insist you proceed them unless you defer to an elder, at which point they smile and sometimes offer the adage, "Old is gold."

It is not strange to see the workers taking small breaks in congregations and sitting beneath the shade before returning to their manual labor. The streets are filled with the usual groups of money exchangers holding large bricks of AFS (Afghan currency) or long strips of calling cards held together like a wallet of children's photographs.

During the evening the locals are often found muttering in small corners and wrapping their heads with scarves as they prepare to catch a small motorcycle taxi back to their homes. Day laborers often spray down walls, streets, vehicles, or other man-made items with a small hose. The night ends with the evening prayer before everyone retires to their beds.

FURTHER READING AND SOURCES

Books

- Malalai Joya, *A Woman Among Warlords: A Woman Among Warlords*, New York: Scribner, 2009.

- Matt Waldman, *Falling Short: Aid Effectiveness in Afghanistan*, Kabul: ACBAR, 2008.

- Kenneth Katzman, *Afghanistan: Post-War Governance, Security, and U.S. Policy*, Washington D.C.: Congressional Research Service, 2008.

- Seth G. Jones, *Counterinsurgency in Afghanistan*, Santa Monica, CA: RAND, 2008.

- *The Afghanistan Compact: Building On Success*, The London Conference on Afghanistan, London, 31 January-1 February, 2006.

- Afghanistan Government, *Strategy for Disbandment of Illegal Armed Groups in Afghanistan (DIAG)*, January 26, 2006.

- Hamish Nixon, *International Assistance and Governance in Afghanistan*, Berlin: Heinrich Boll Foundation, 2007.

- NATO, *ISAF PRT Handbook*, 3rd Ed. February 2007.

- Sarah Chayes, *The Punishment of Virtue: Inside Afghanistan After the Taliban*, New York: Penguin Press, 2006.

- Steve Coll, *Ghost Wars: The Secret History of the CIA, Afghanistan, and Bin Laden, From the Soviet Invasion to September 10, 2001*, New York: Penguin Press, 2004.

- Louis Dupree, *Afghanistan*, Princeton: Princeton University Press, 1979.

- Edward R. Girardet, *Afghanistan: The Soviet War*. New Delhi, India: Selectbook Service Syndicate, 1985.

- Edward Girardet and Jonathan Walter, *Afghanistan: Essential Field Guides to Humanitarian and Conflict Zones*, CROSSLINES Publication Ltd, 1998 and 2004. www.crosslinesguides.com

- Larry Goodson, *Afghanistan's Endless War: State Failure, Regional Politics, and the Rise of the Taliban*, Seattle: University of Washington Press, 2001.

- Michael Griffin, *Reaping the Whirlwind: The Taliban Movement in Afghanistan*, London: Pluto Press, 2001.

- Ben Macintyre, *The Man Who Would Be King: The First American in Afghanistan*, New York: Farrar, Straus and Giroux, 2005.

- Greg Mortenson, *Three Cups of Tea: One Man's Mission to Promote Peace...One School at a Time*, New York: Penguin Books, 2006. (excellent understanding of how to succeed with the people and culture)

- Sean Naylor, *Not a Good Day to Die: The Untold Story of Operation Anaconda*, London: Penquin/Michael Joseph, 2005.

- Ahmed Rashid, *Descent into Chaos: The United States and the Future of Nation Building in Afghanistan, Pakistan, and Central Asia*, New York: Viking Press, 2008.

- Ahmed Rashid, *Taliban: Militant Islam, Oil and Fundamentalism in Central Asia*, New Haven: Yale University Press, 2000.

- Barnett Rubin, *The Fragmentation of Afghanistan*, New Haven: Yale University Press, 2001.

Articles

- Thomas Schweich, "Is Afghanistan a Narco-State?" *New York Times Magazine*, July 27, 2008.

- Hamed Karzai, *The Afghanistan National Development Strategy*, 2006, www.reliefweb.int/rw/RWFiles2006.nsf/ dbc12f058effd2dac125749600457fd4/c125723c004042d7c12573a a00474d8b/$FILE/unama-afg-30jan2.pdf

- Raphy Favre, *Potential Analysis of the Eastern Region and Nangarhar Province and Implication in Programming,* September 2005, http://aizon.org/Nangarhar%20Potential%20Analysis.pdf

- G.H. Orris and J.D. Bliss (eds), *Mines and Mineral Occurrences of Afghanistan,* open-file report 02-110, U S .Geological Survey, US Department of the Interior, 2002.

- Barnett Rubin, "Afghanistan's Uncertain Transition from Turmoil to Normalcy," *Council Special Report*, No. 12, March 2007.

- Andrew Wilder, "Cops or Robbers: The Struggle to Reform the Afghan National Police," *Afghan Research and Evaluation Unit*, July 2007, www.areu.org.af/index. php?option=com_docman&task=doc_download&gid=523

Websites

- Afghanistan Research and Evaluation Unit (publishes the *Afghanistan A to Z guide)*, www.areu.org.af/index.php?option=com_frontpage&Itemid=25

- Afghanistan Information Management Services, *www.aims.org.af*

- Afghanistan Online (Links to Official IRA and embassy websites), *www.afghan-web.com/politics*

- Naval Postgraduate School Program for Culture and Conflict Studies, *www.nps.edu/Programs/CCS/index.html*

- USAID, *www.usaid.gov/locations/asia/countries/afghanistan*

www.ingramcontent.com/pod-product-compliance
Lightning Source LLC
Chambersburg PA
CBHW042327150426
43193CB00001B/9